DRIVE BY SHOOTING

Max Forsythe

Published by Booth-Clibborn Editions

To create something of value you have to have strong beliefs.

Even, one could say, prejudices. Throughout Max's photographic career he's certainly displayed quite a few.

Mostly, they've been about colour.

Unadulterated, vibrant, sometimes enhanced, but always powerful. Not that he's a stranger to black and white. Far from it, but I guess his heart lies in capturing that iconic image with a blast of colour. He's even published a stunning collection of pictures exploring the subject entitled Colour Prejudice.

Most photographers seeking recognition would eschew that view and retreat to the security and respectability of the monochromatic image.

Max has never been one to follow respectability or a popular view. He follows his own. Fashionable or not. Life happens in colour, so do his pictures.

It's this desire to show us the world as a constantly evolving canvas that has lead Max to Drive by Shooting. It's a world that continually evolves before our eyes. Especially as we drive, ride, fly by it. He makes us look again at the fascinating jumble of images framed, not so much by the camera, but by the window of the vehicle he's in.

Our lives are constantly framed by events, often out of our control. Here they're framed by the incidental nature of a journey.

Drive by Shooting captures those fleeting moments in all their vivid intensity.

Humorous, odd, poetic, silly and weird.

It reminds us life doesn't happen in black and white. It happens in colour and sadly, for so many, it passes them by.

John Hegarty

Max Forsythe grew up in Northern Ireland and studied Graphic Design at Belfast College of Art. From there he went to the London College of Printing and then started a career in advertising as an Art Director at some of Londons most creative agencies.

In 1972 Max switched to photography and since then has worked mainly for advertising specializing in location and reportage.

Travel has given him the opportunity to persue his personal projects.

Max has always extolled the virtues of colour in photography even when it was deeply unfashionable in the 70's and 80's. He often shoots in countries that are unashamed in their approach to and use of colour, like Ireland, Morocco and the Carribean and published a limited edition book of these pictures called Colour Prejudice.

Max has won many awards including four D&AD Silvers and a Bronze Lion for Directing at Cannes.

His first one man show was held at Hamiltons Gallery , London in 1984 where he also exhibited in 1992.

His show Incidental Images was on display at The Association of Photographers Gallery, London in 2001 and Drive by Shooting was first exhibited at the Lupe Gallery London in 2004.

Max has also participated in a number of group shows.

His work is in the collections of The Royal Photographic Society and The National Museum of Photography.

He lives in Richmond, London with his wife Jane who is also his Producer.

Max's future projects include a book on Ireland and a second edition of Colour Prejudice.

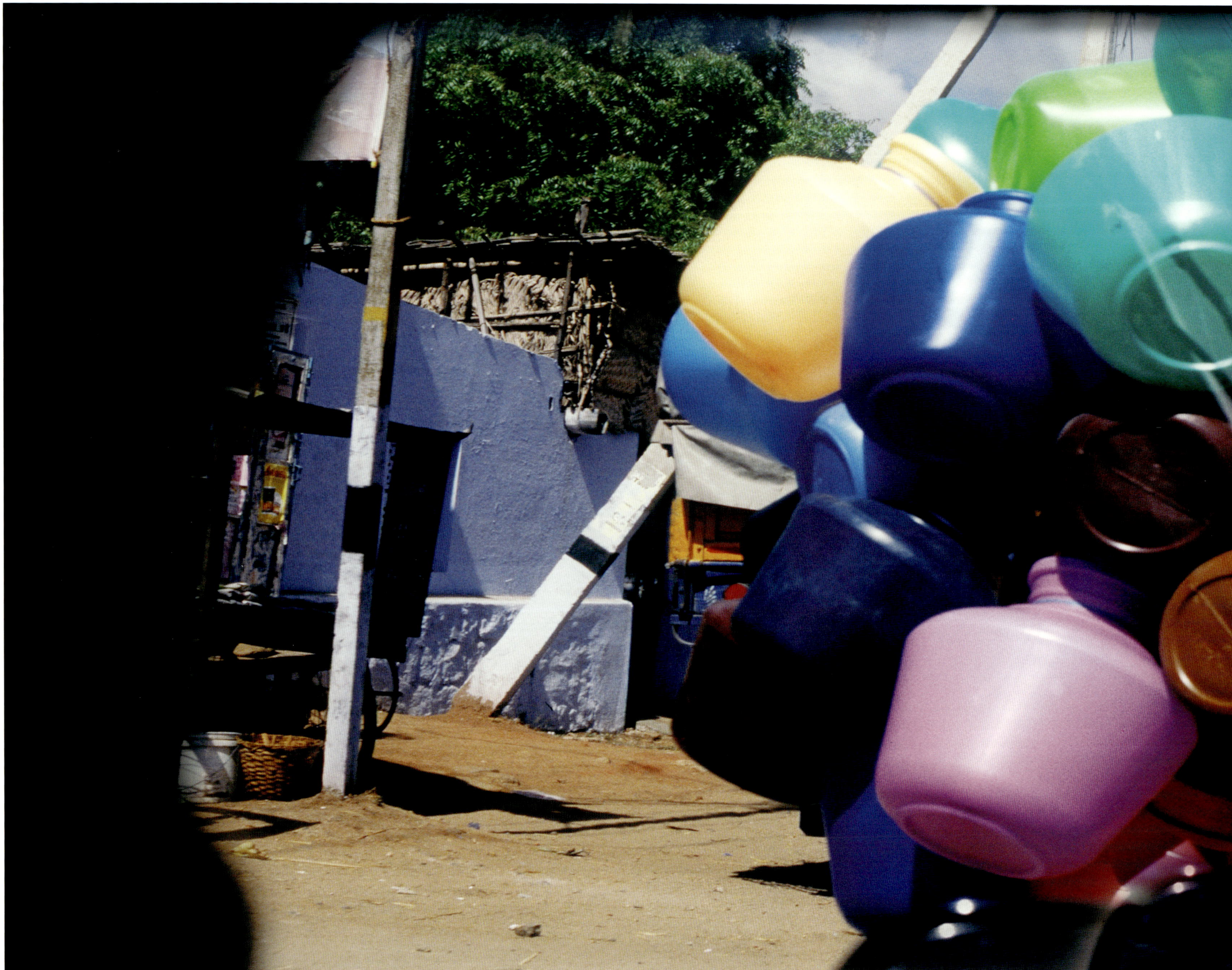

Overtaking a heavily laden bicycle on the road to Madurai, Southern India

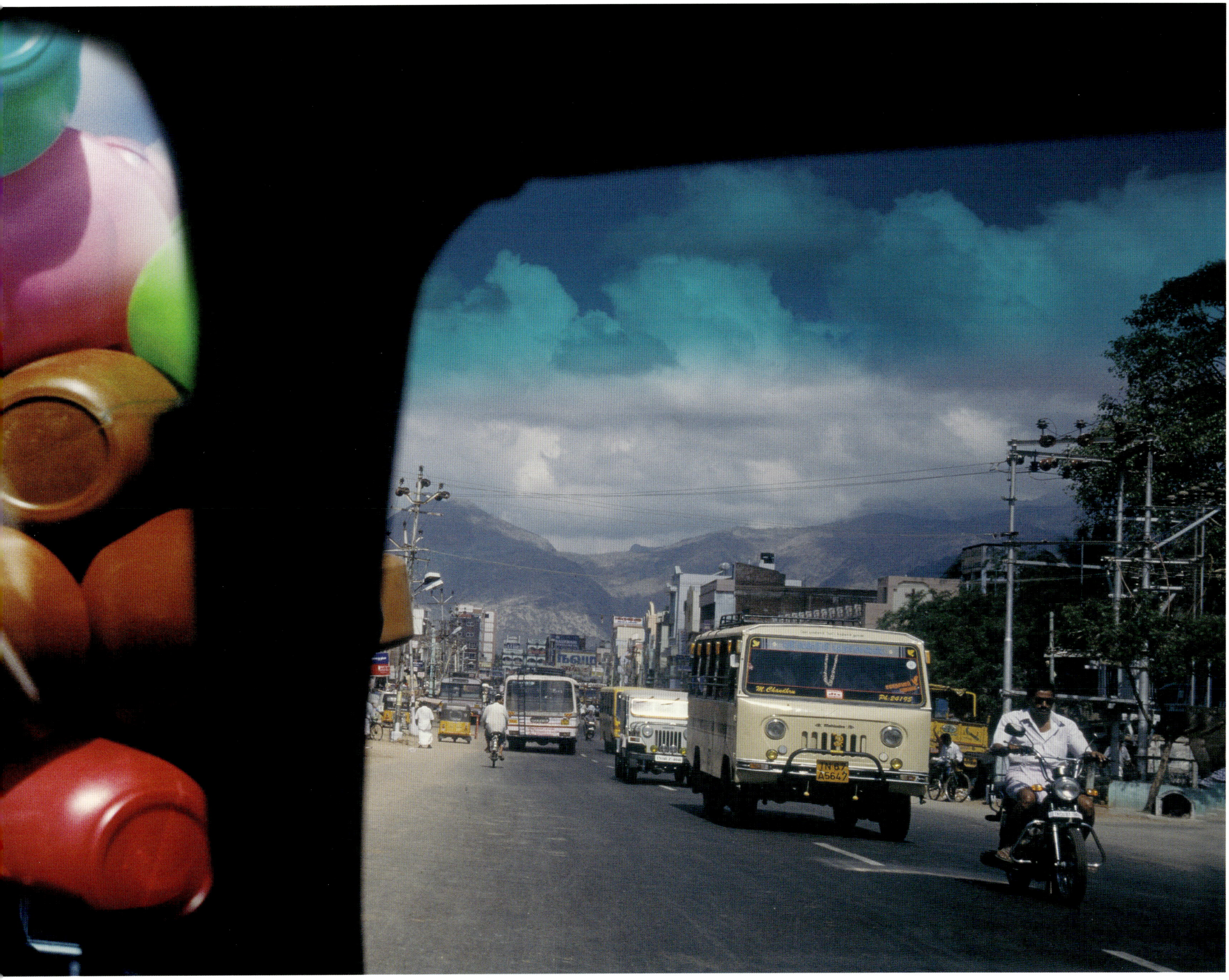
M. Chandhru
Ph. 24195
TN 67
A5647

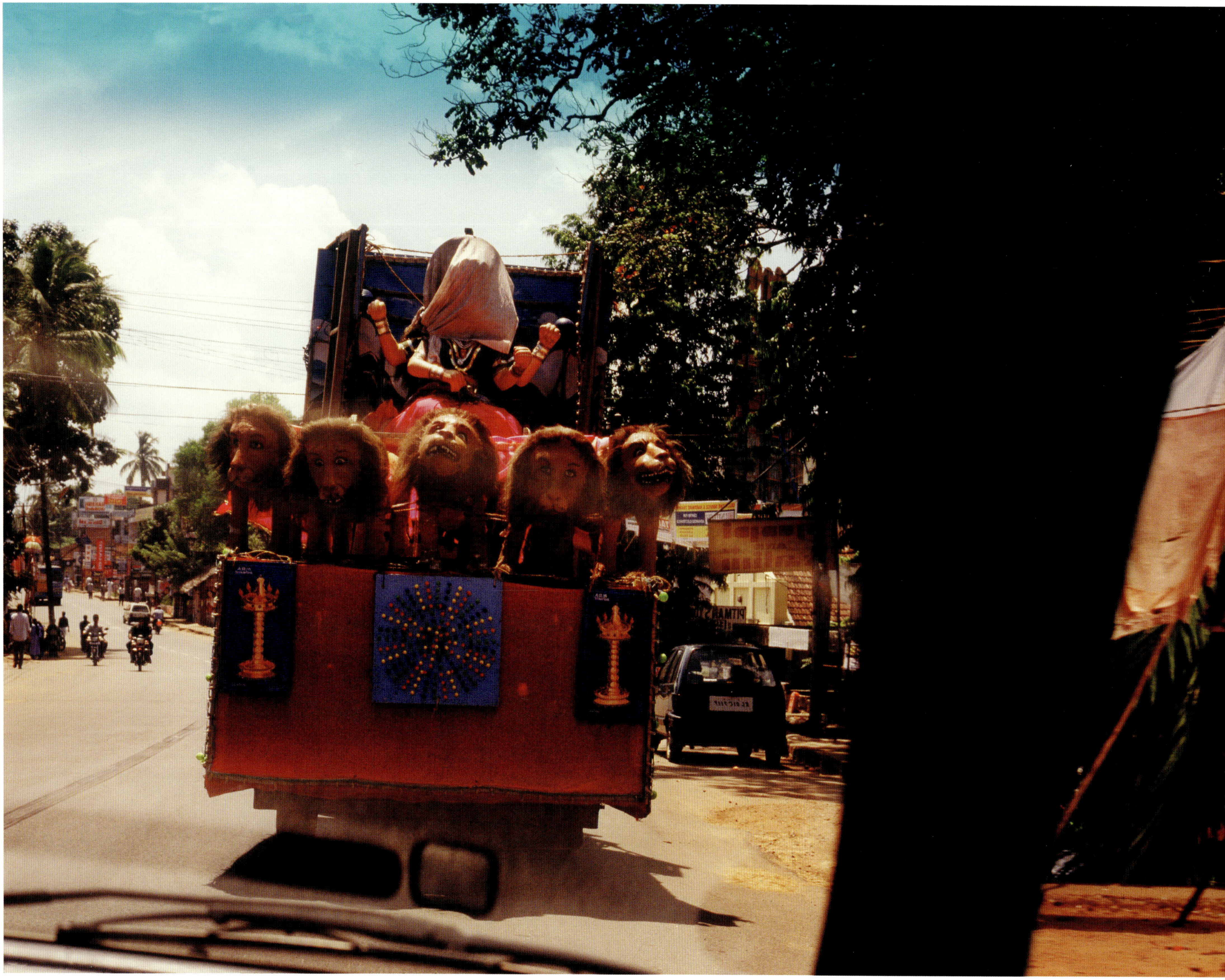

Carnival truck on a road in Kerala India

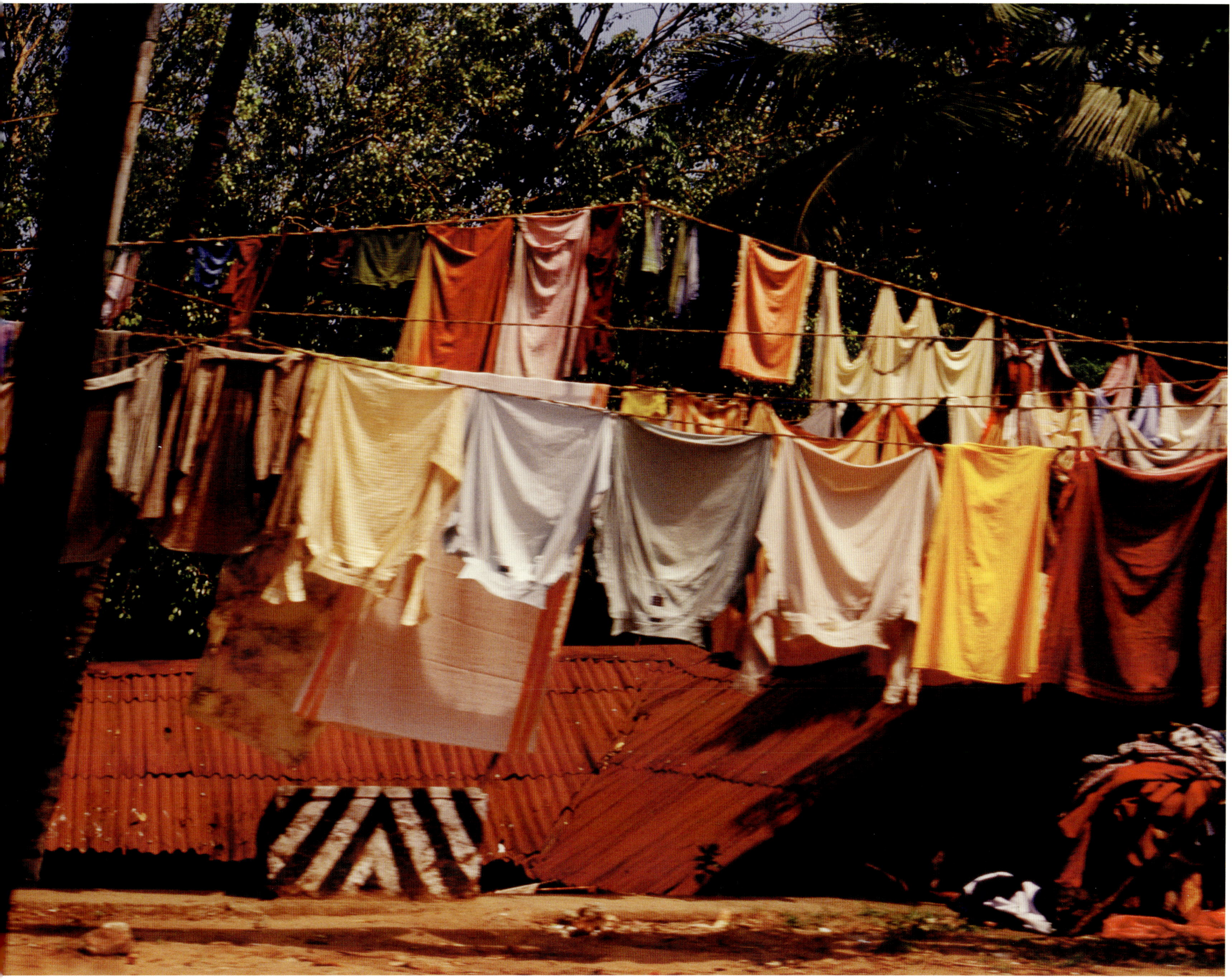

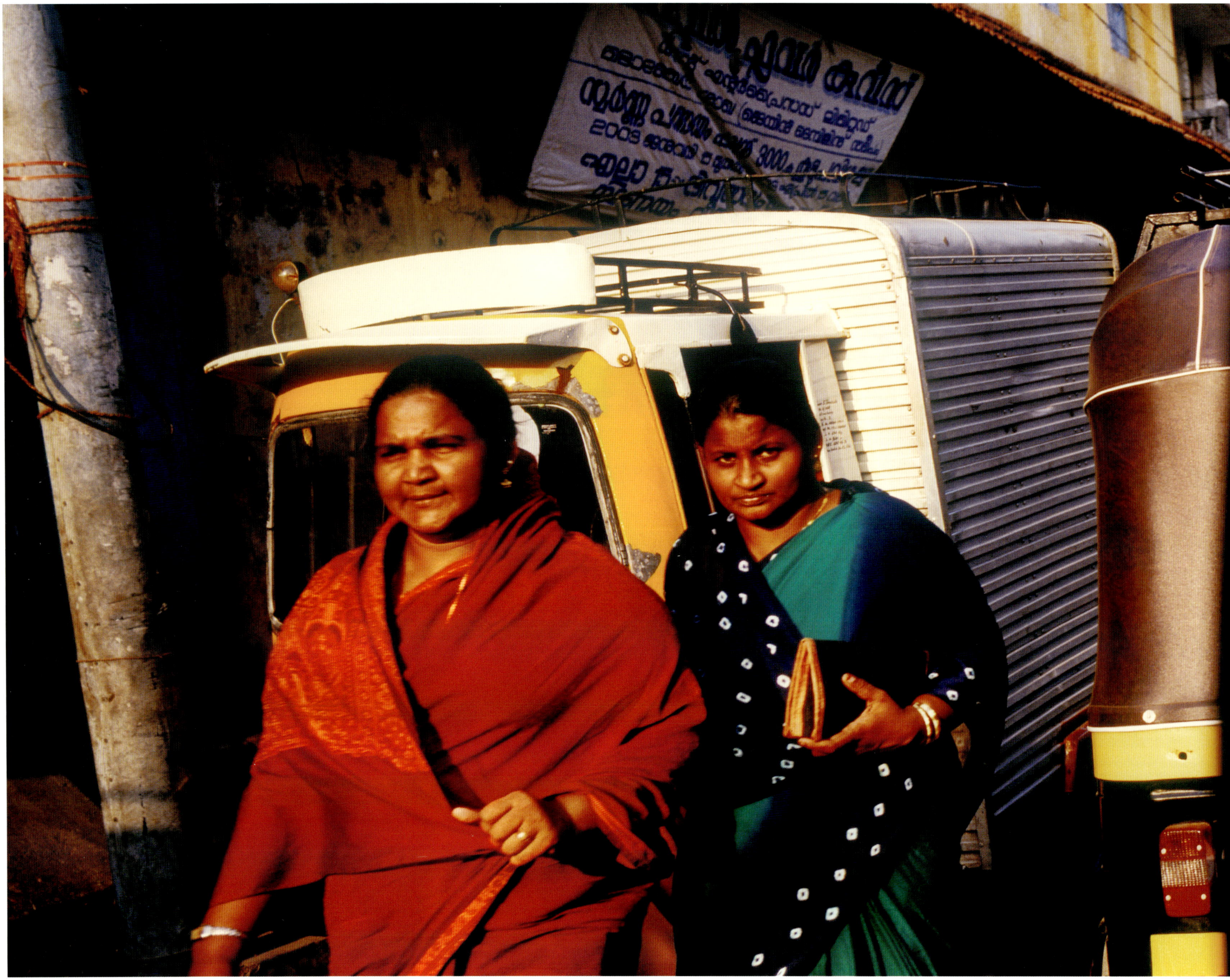

The back streets of the Spice Markets, Cochin, India

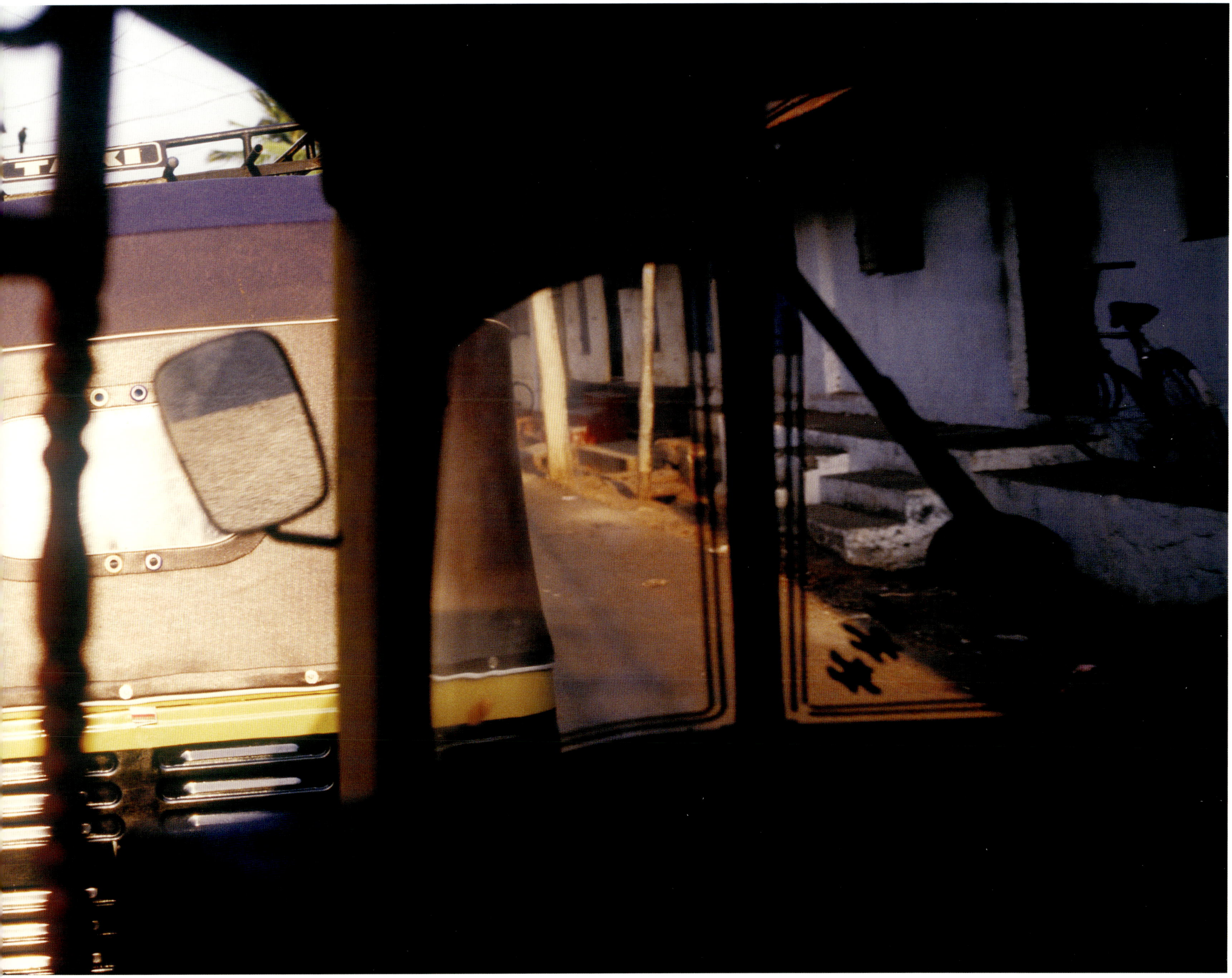

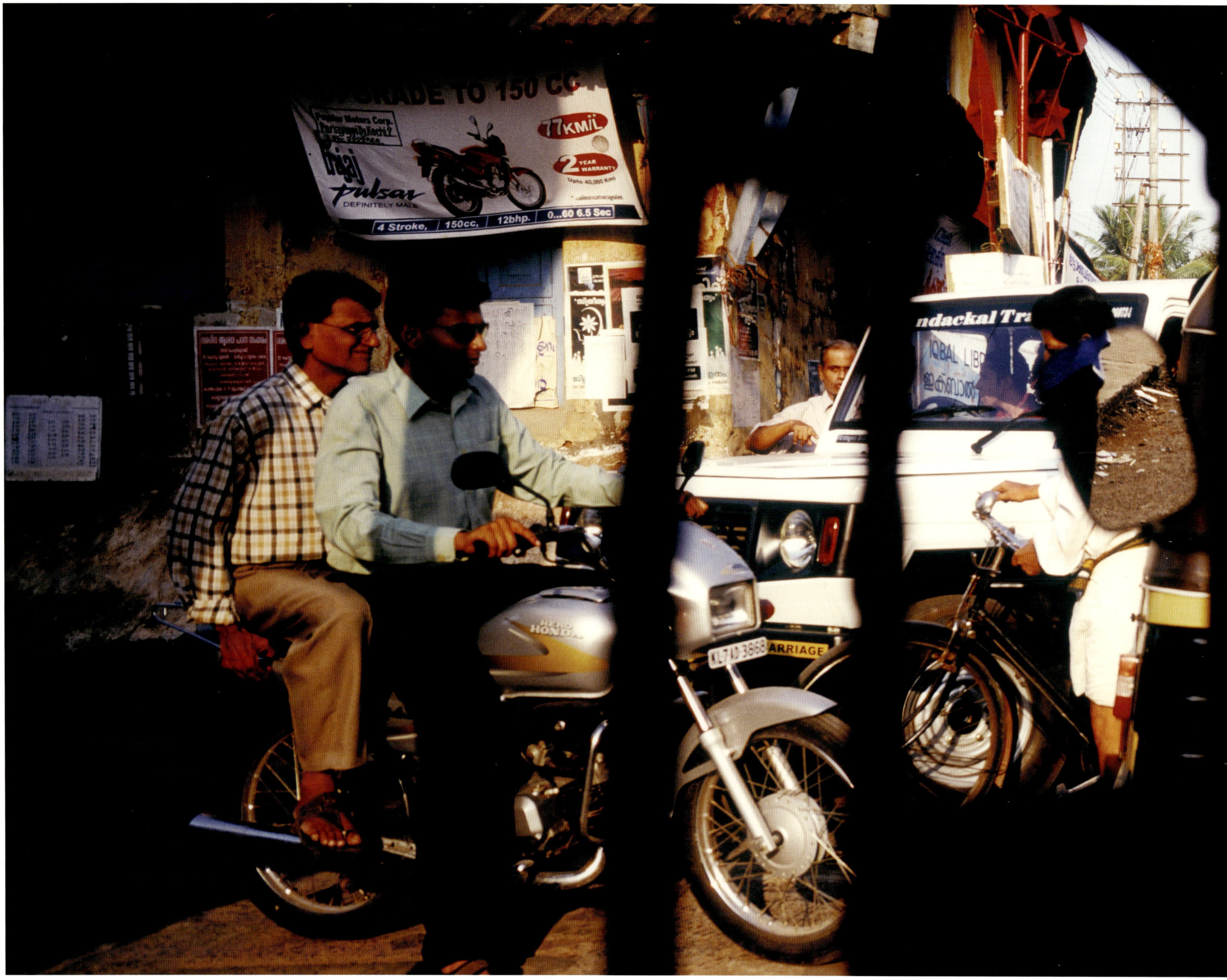

The back streets of Cochin, India

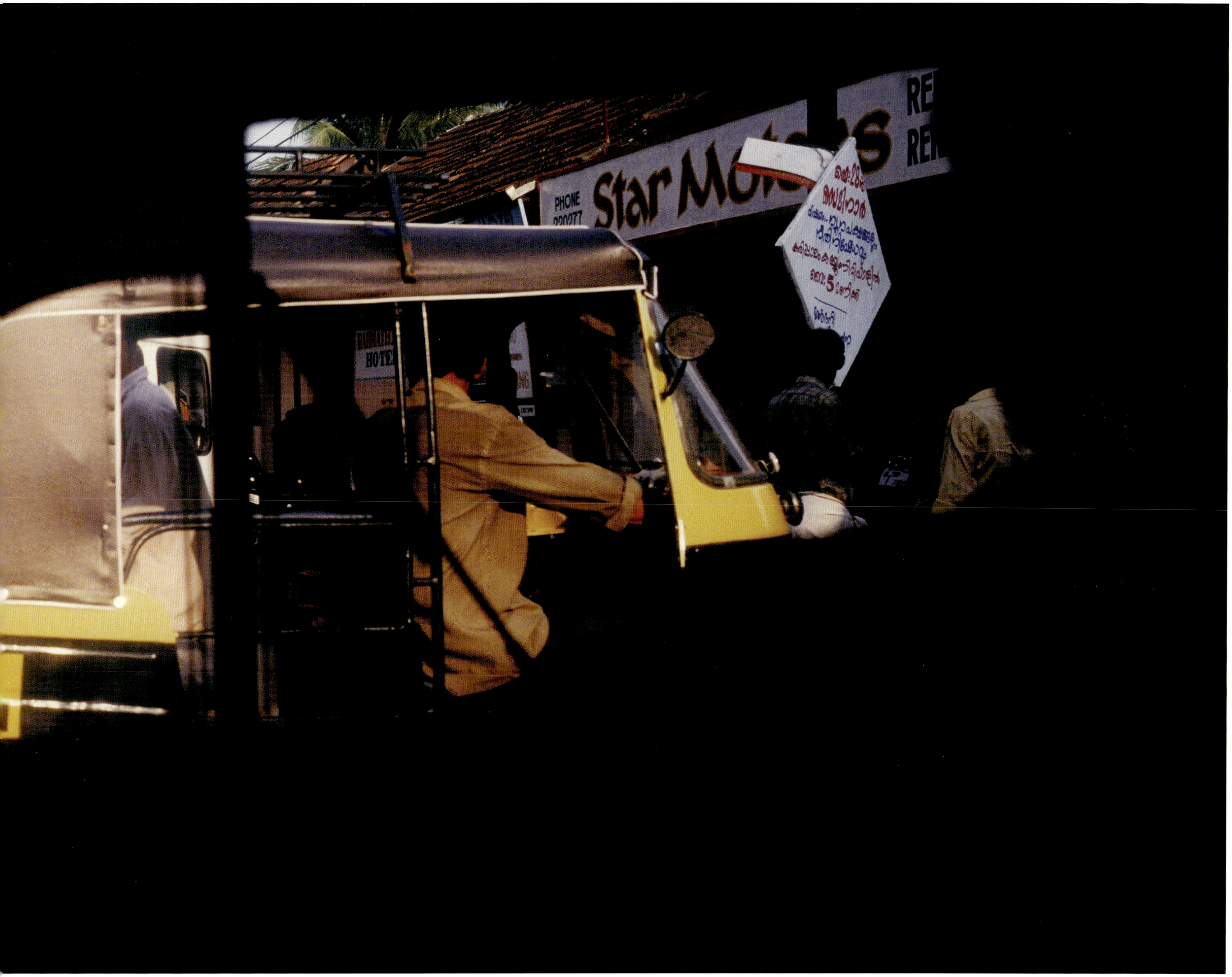
PHONE
Star

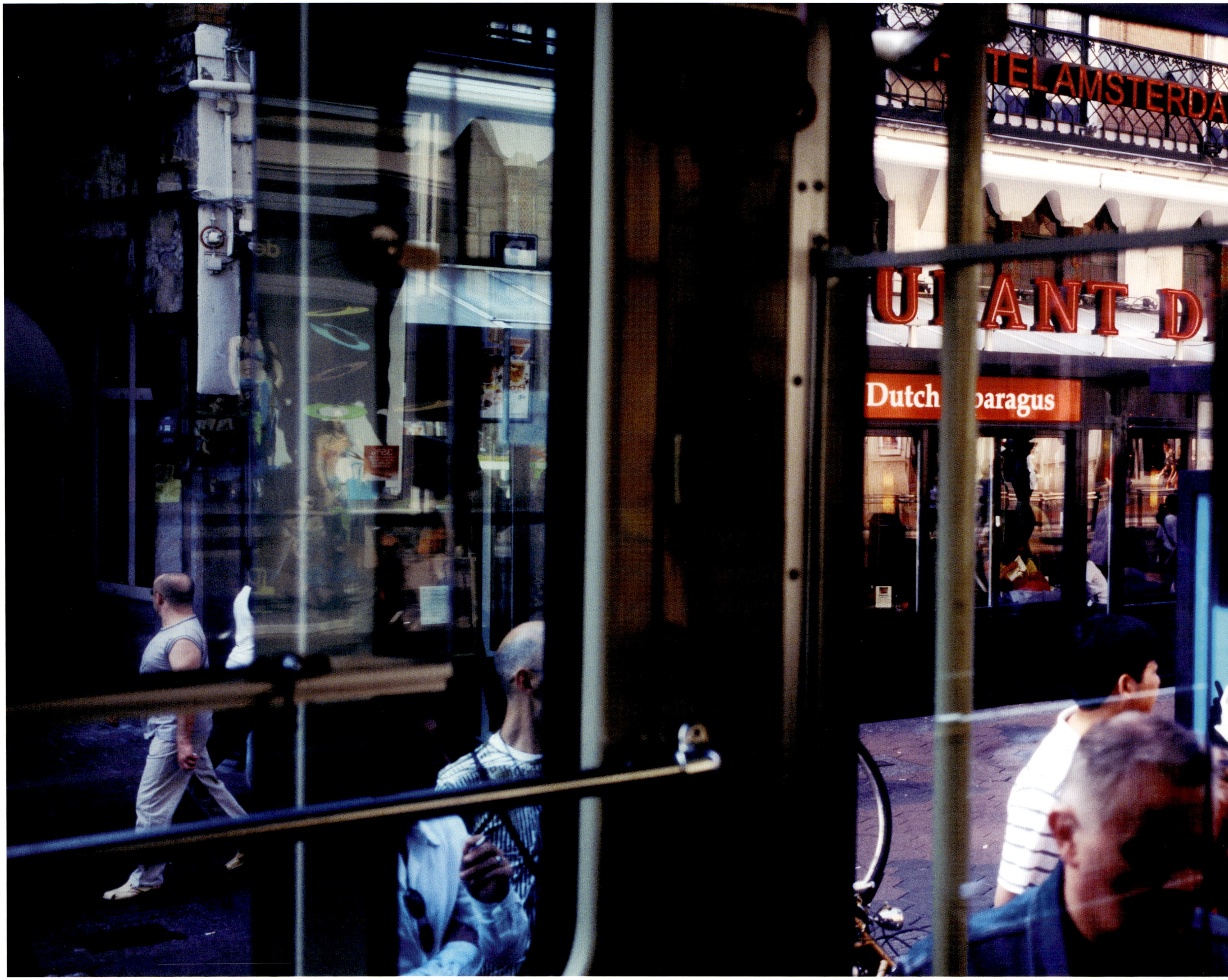

A tram in Amsterdam

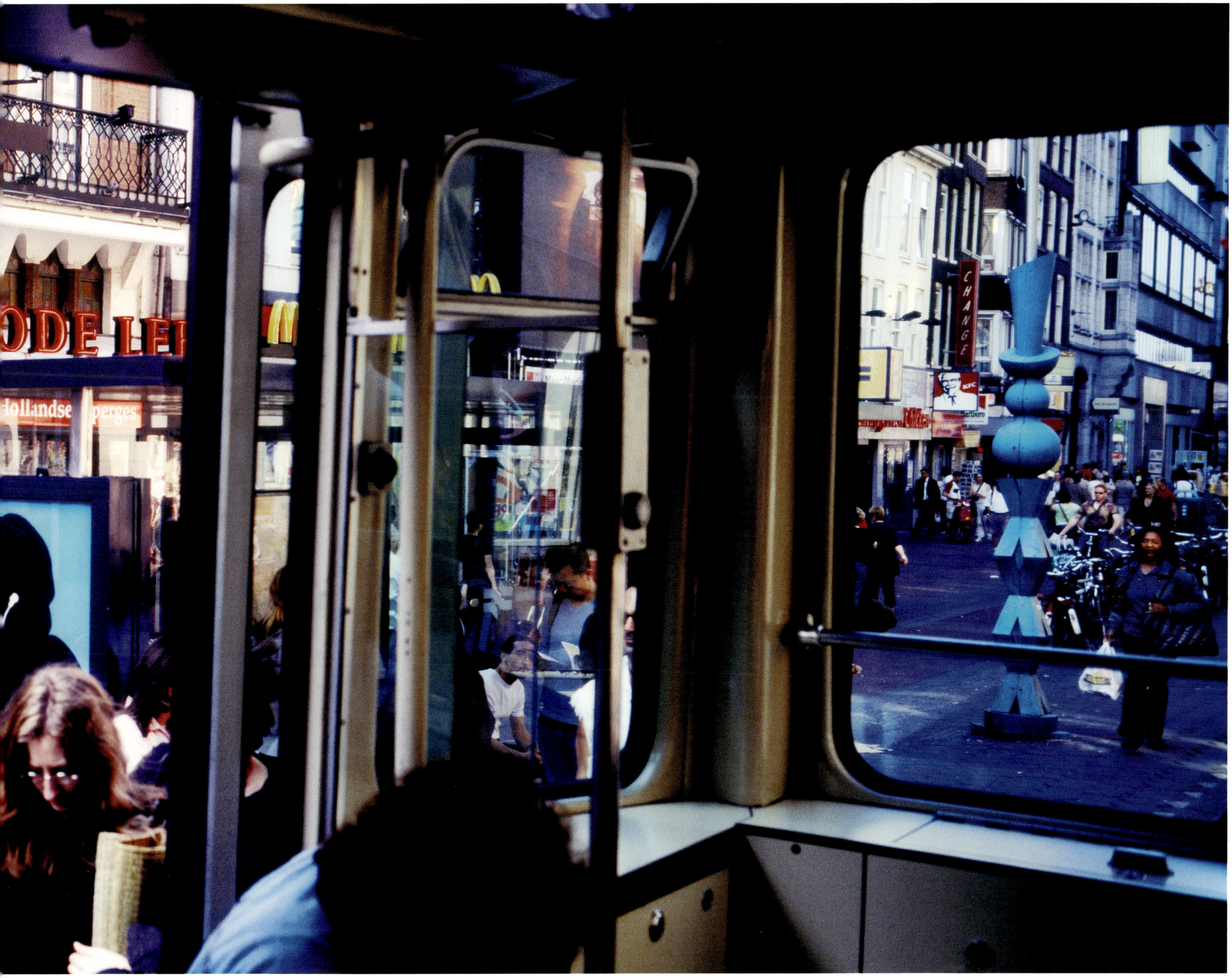
CHANGE
KFC

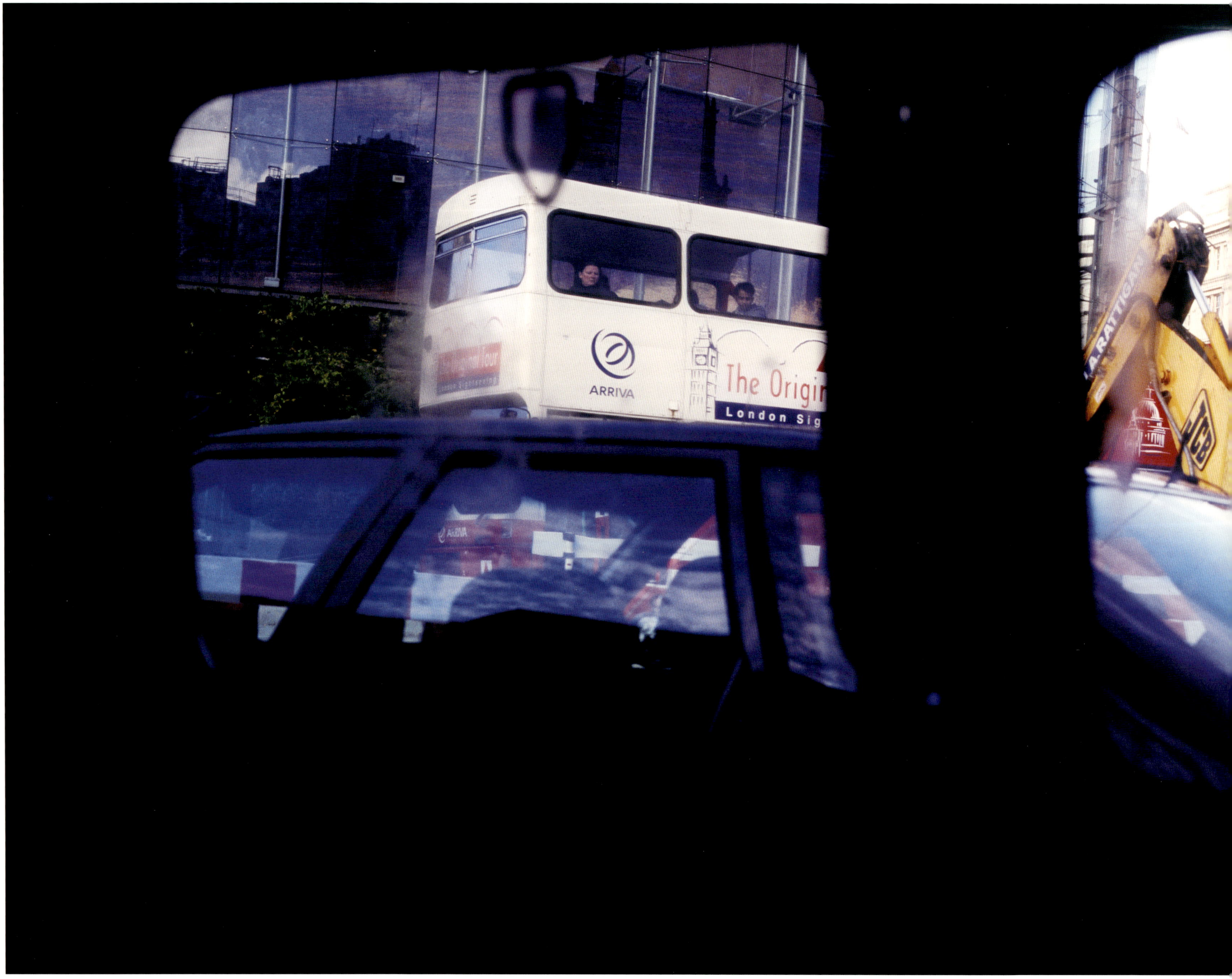

Waterloo roundabout London

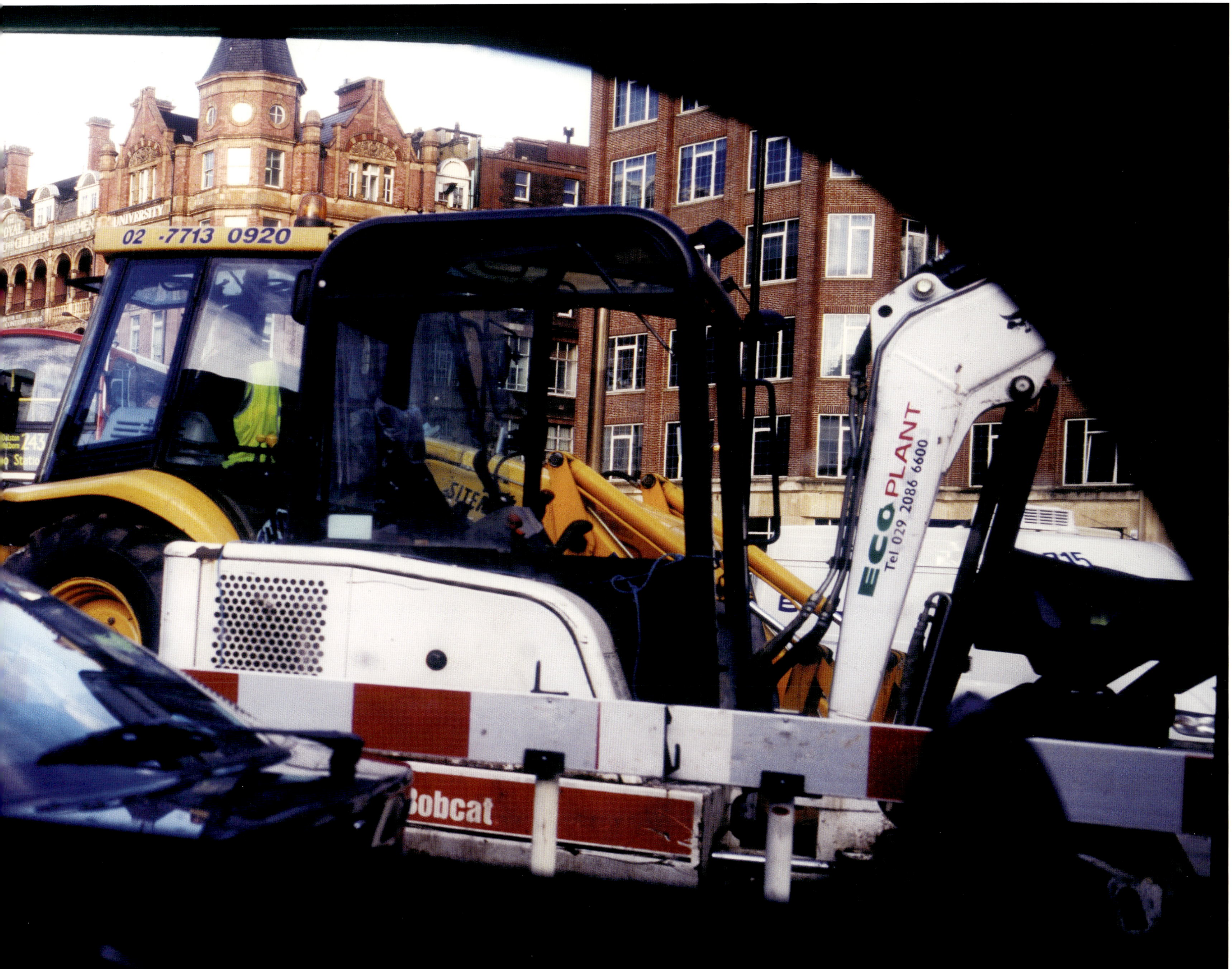
UNIVERSITY
02 ·7713 0920
ECO PLANT
Tel 029 2086 6600
Bobcat

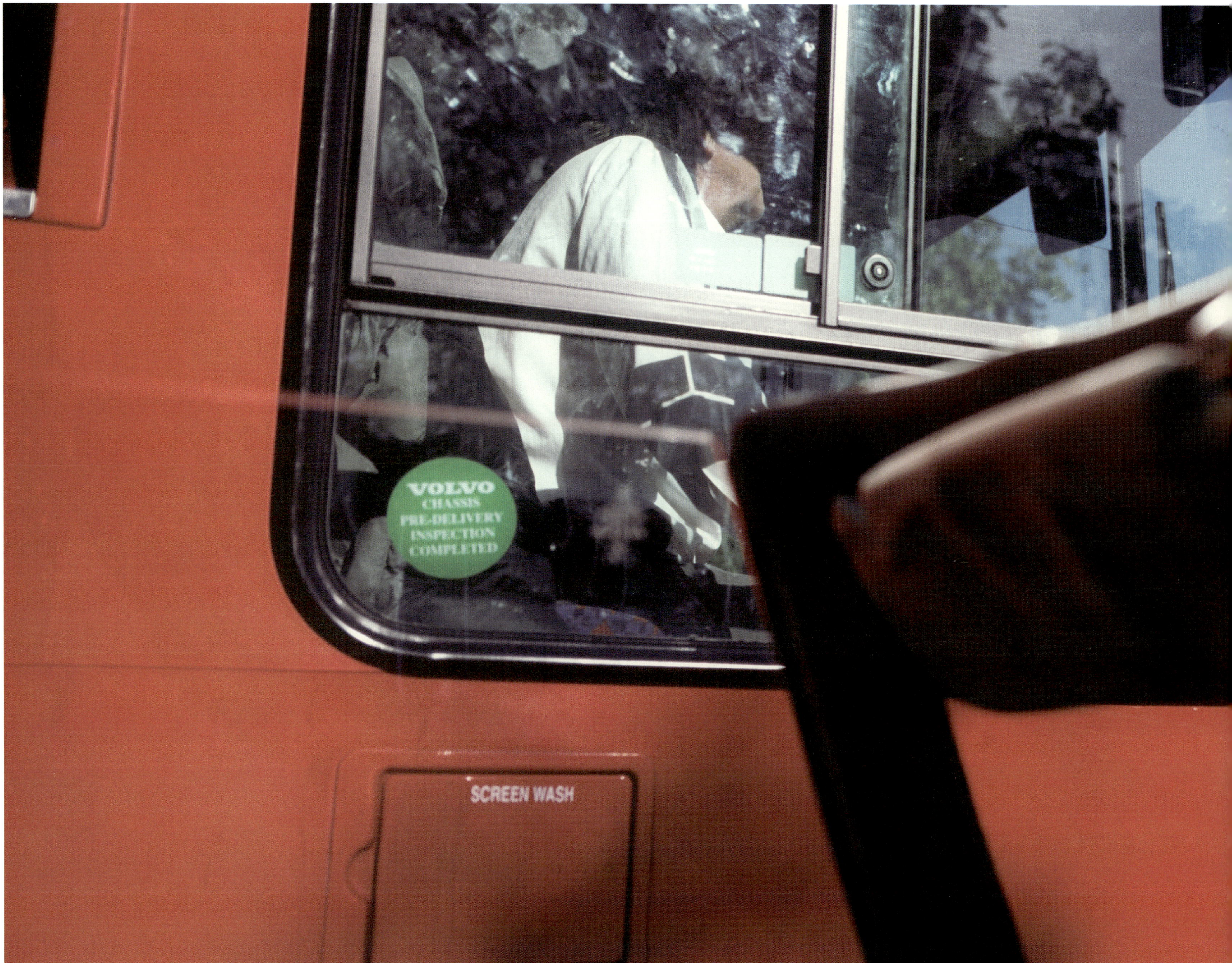

Traffic in Parliament Square, London

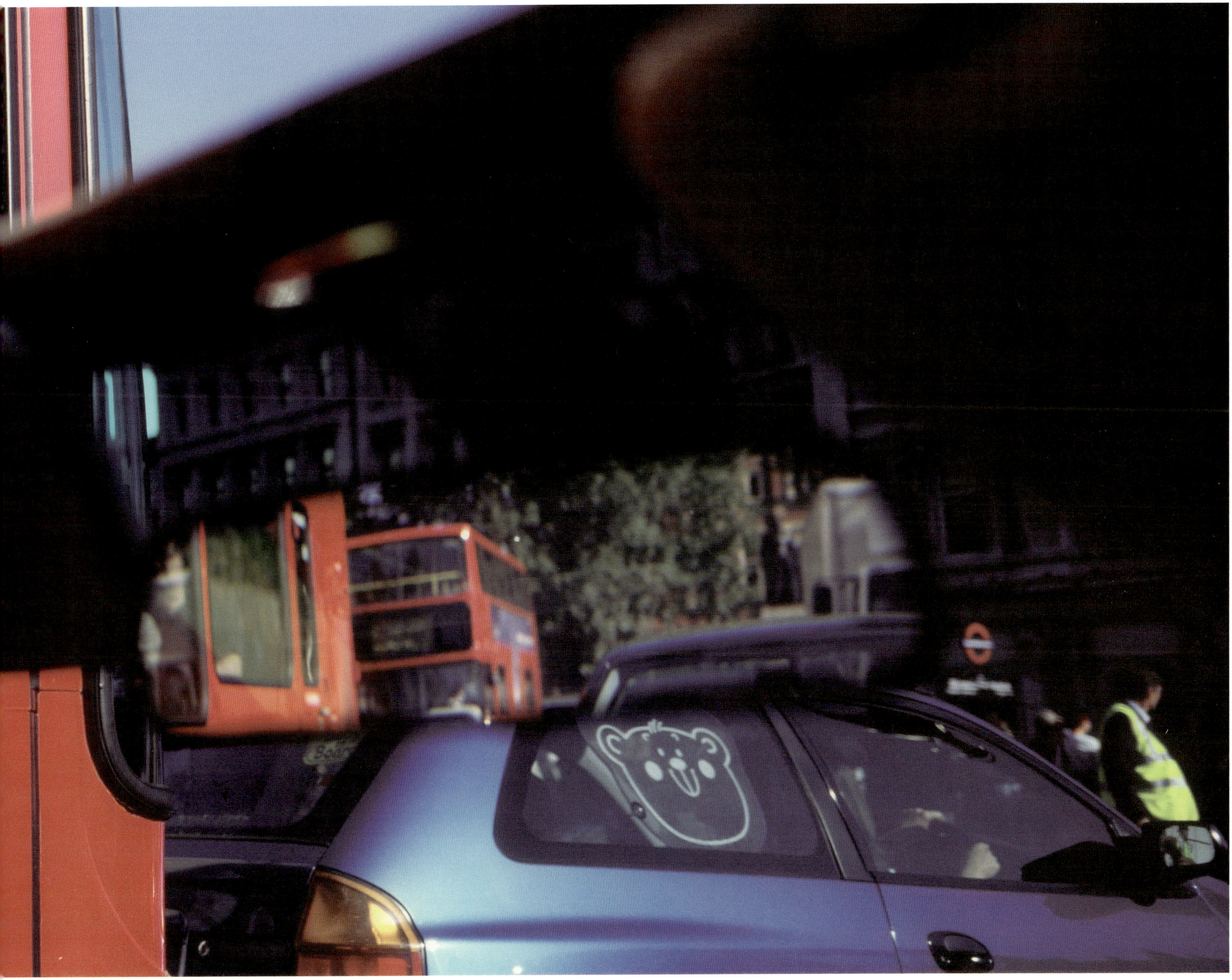

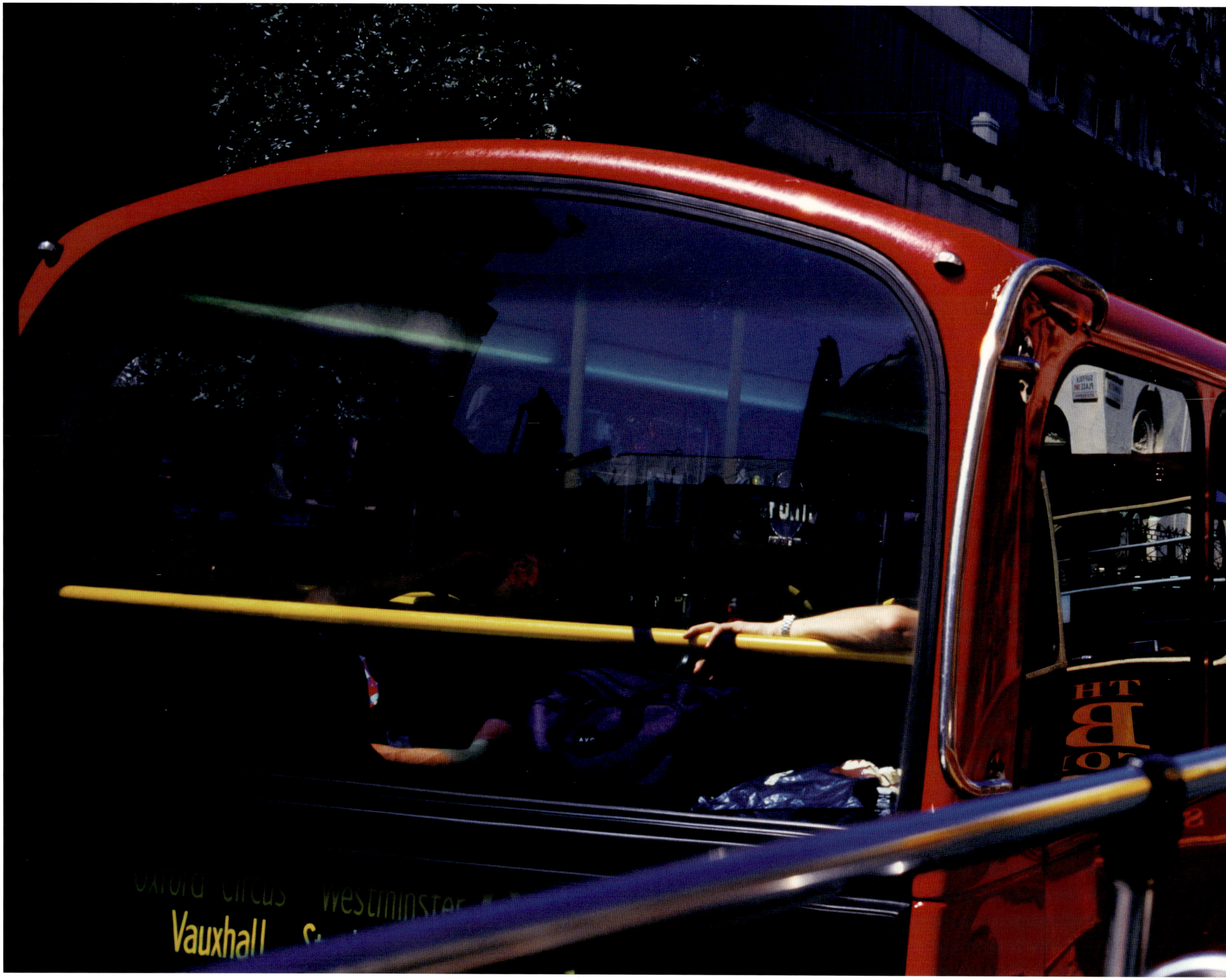

On top of the tour bus in Regent Street, London

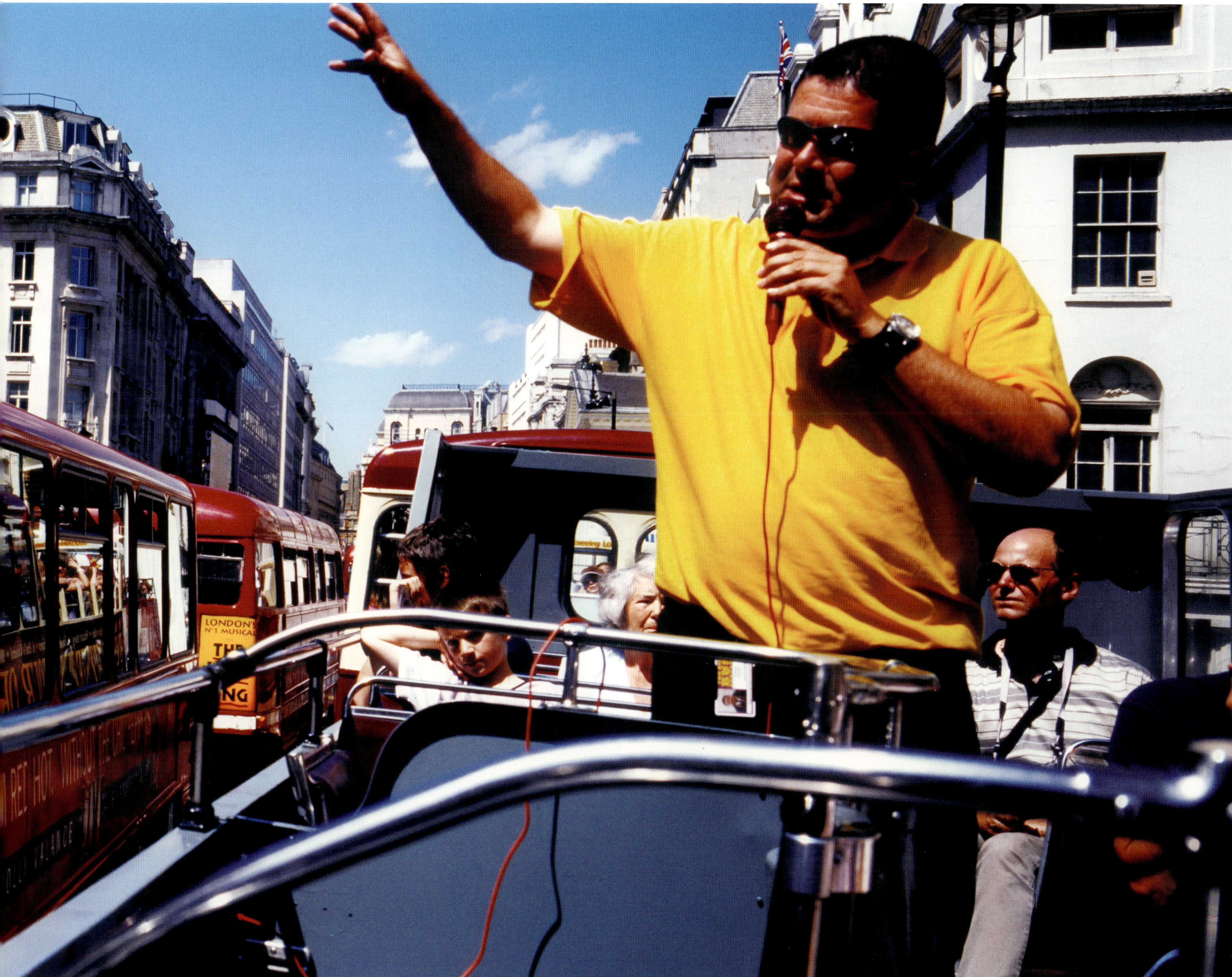
LONDON'S

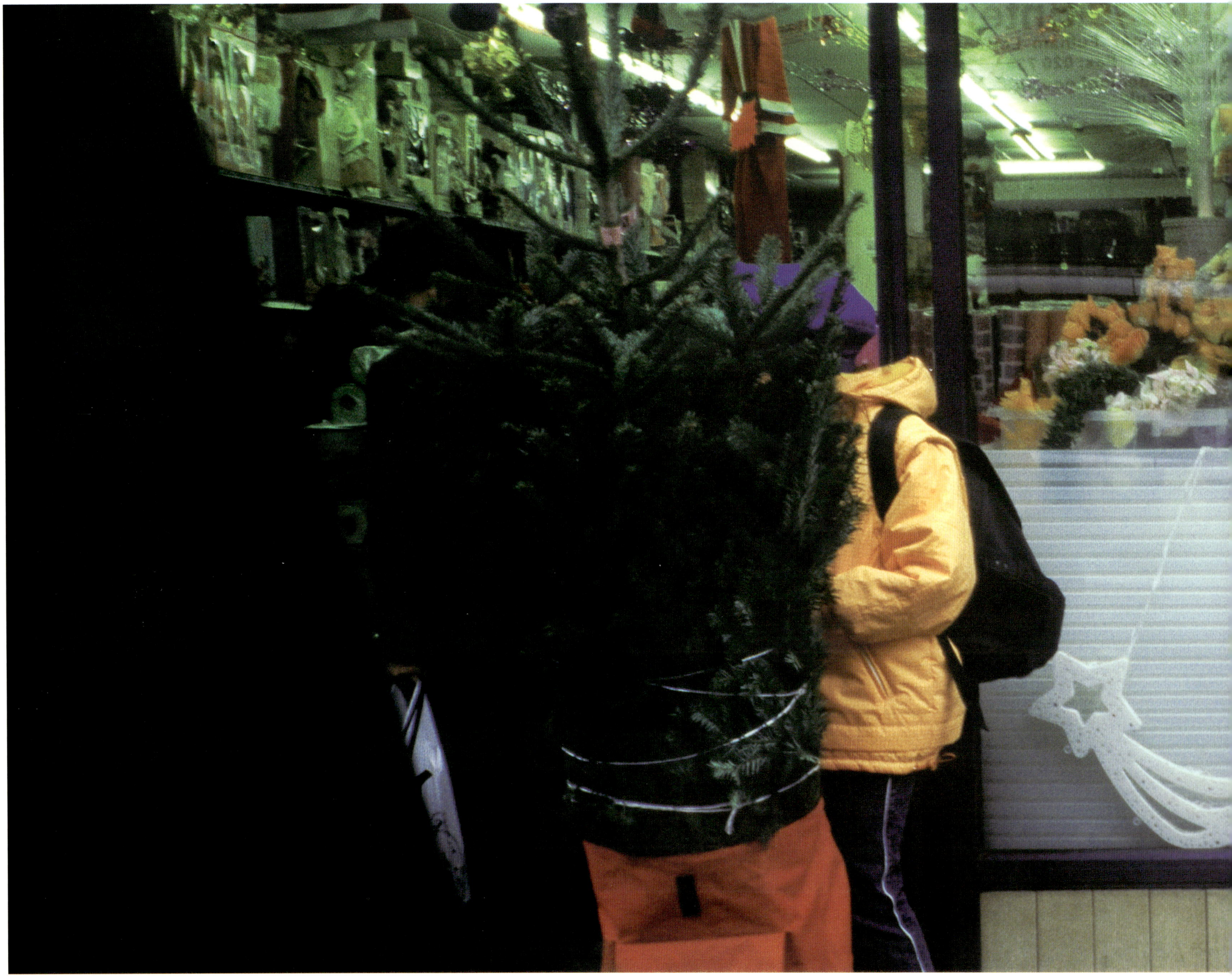

Christmas in North End Road, London

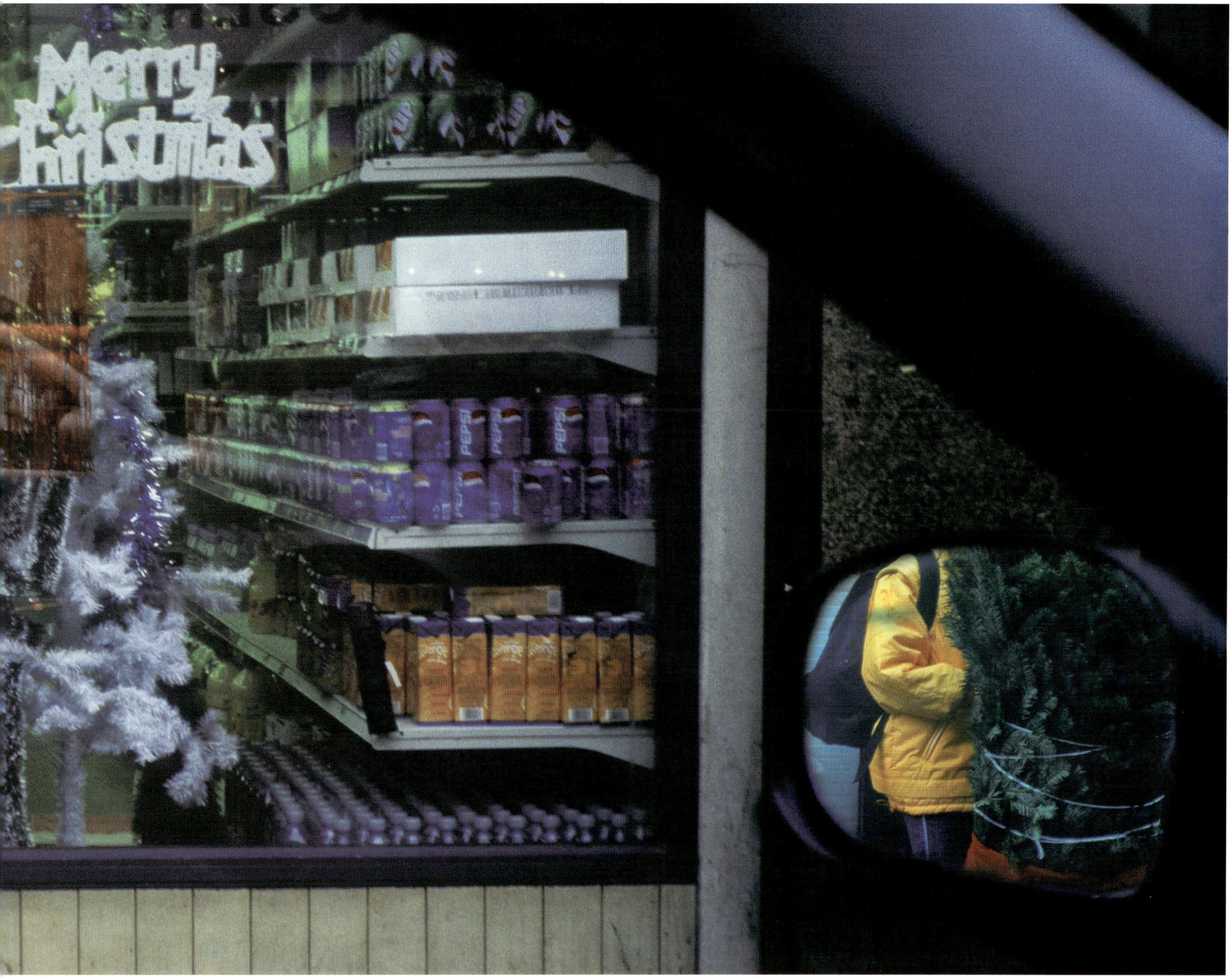
Merry Christmas
PEPSI

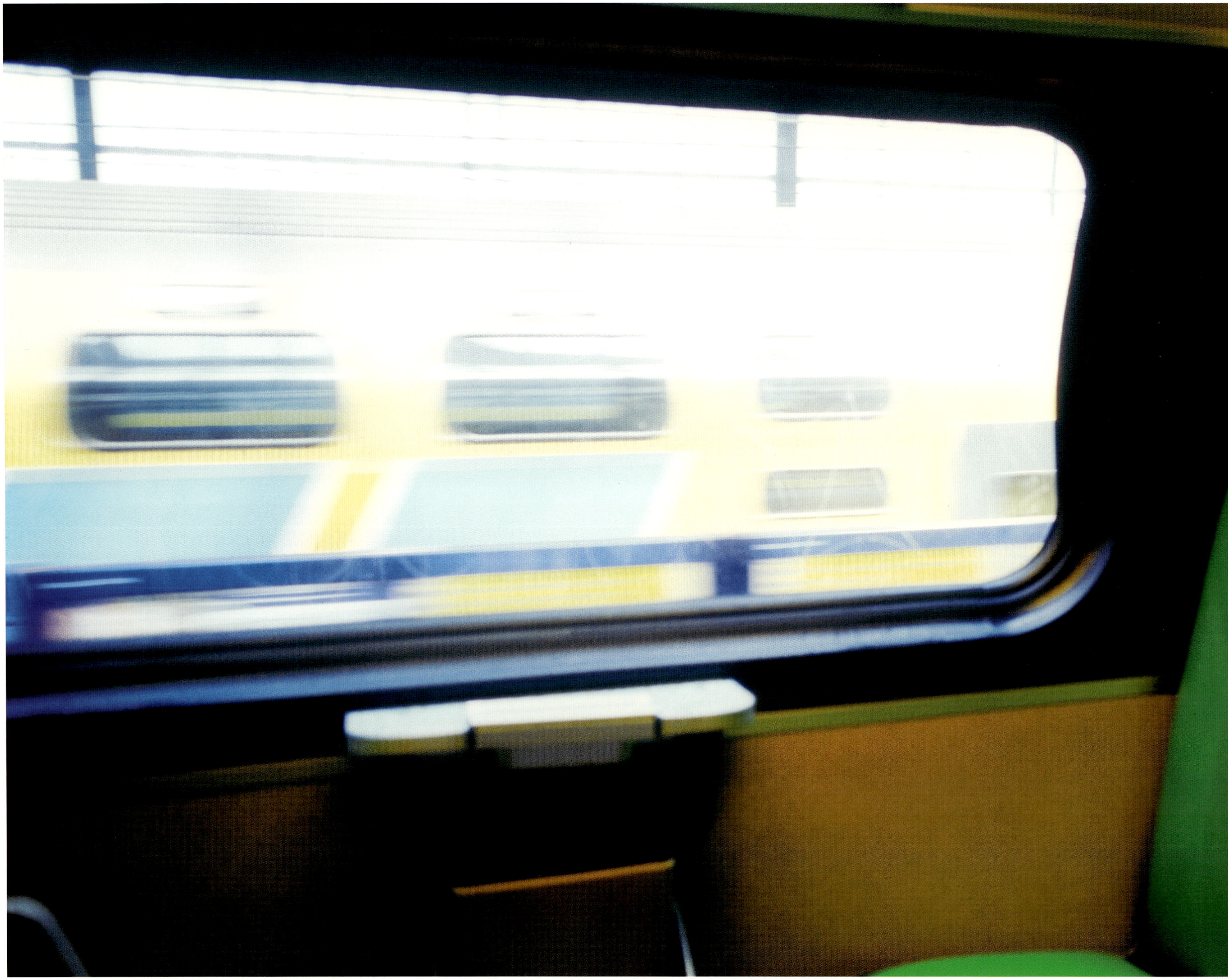

On the tram from Schiphol Airport, Holland

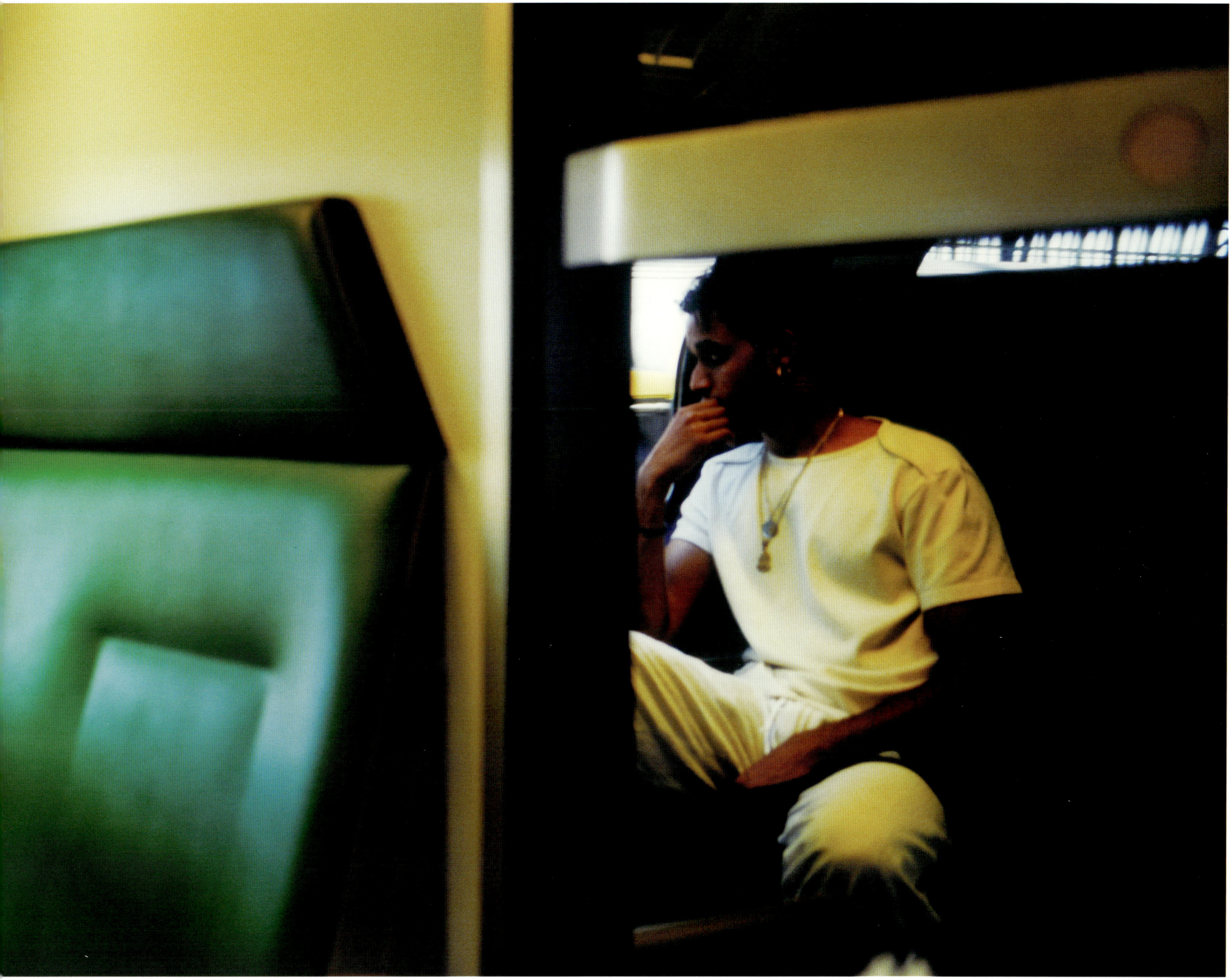

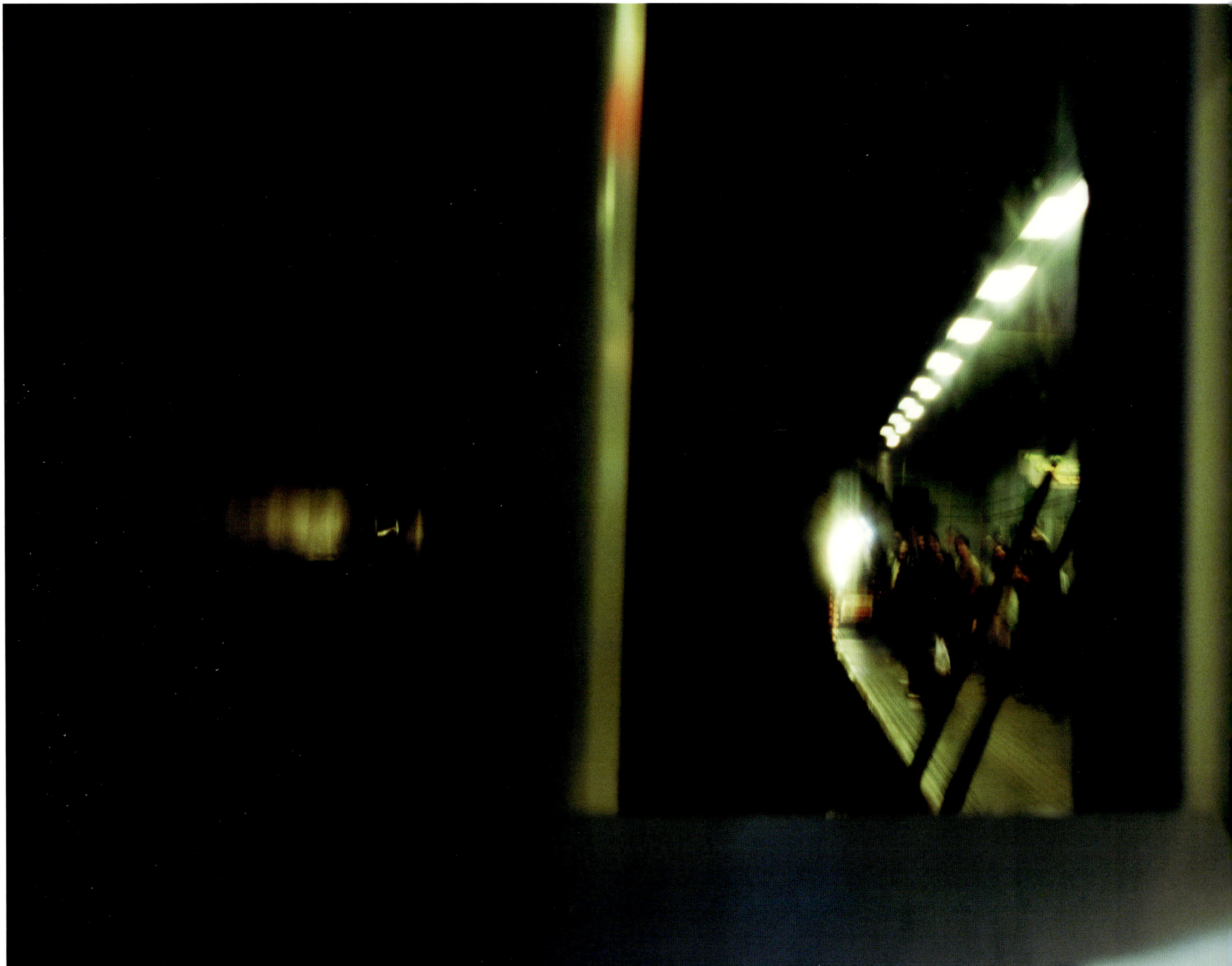

The Docklands Light Railway, London

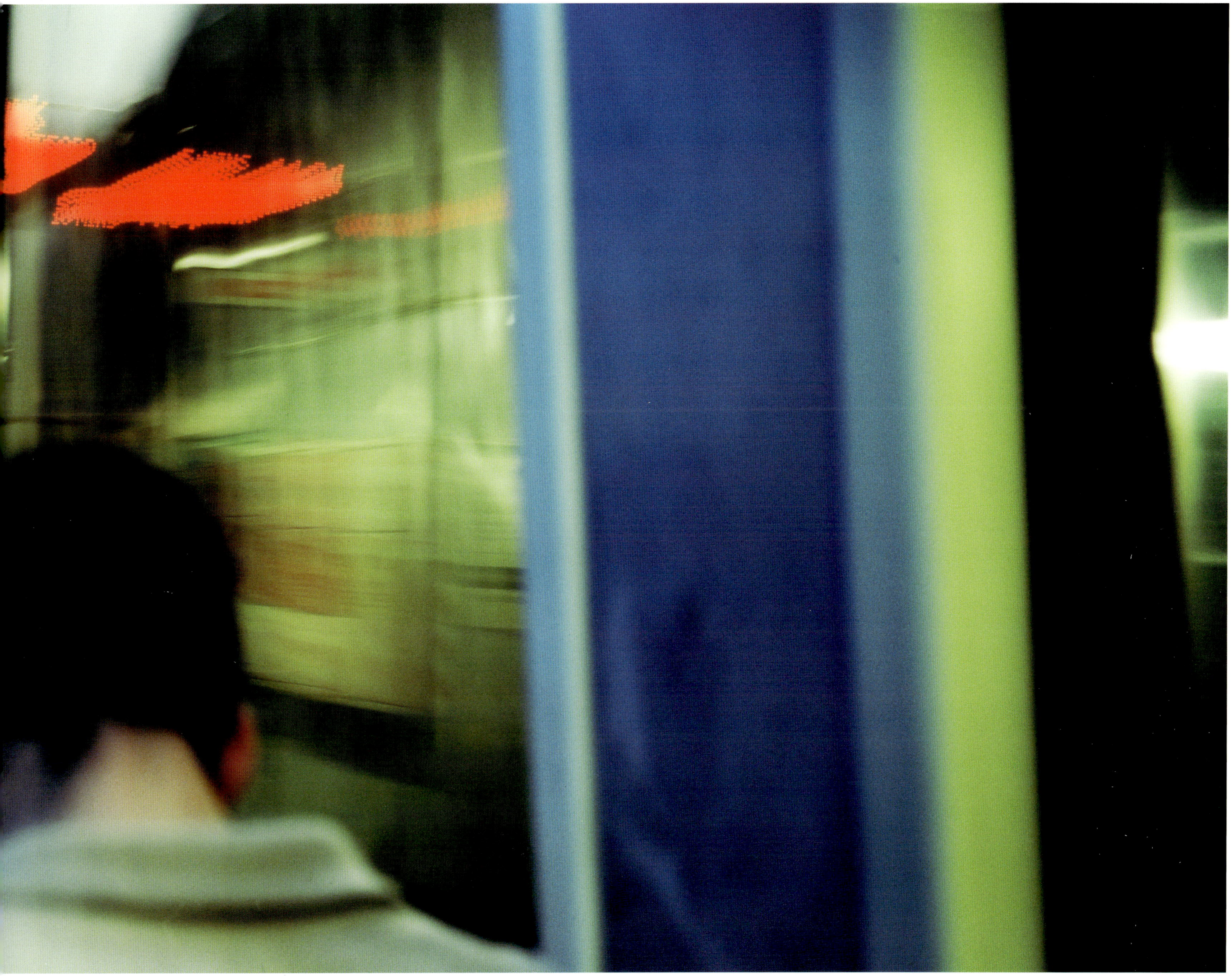

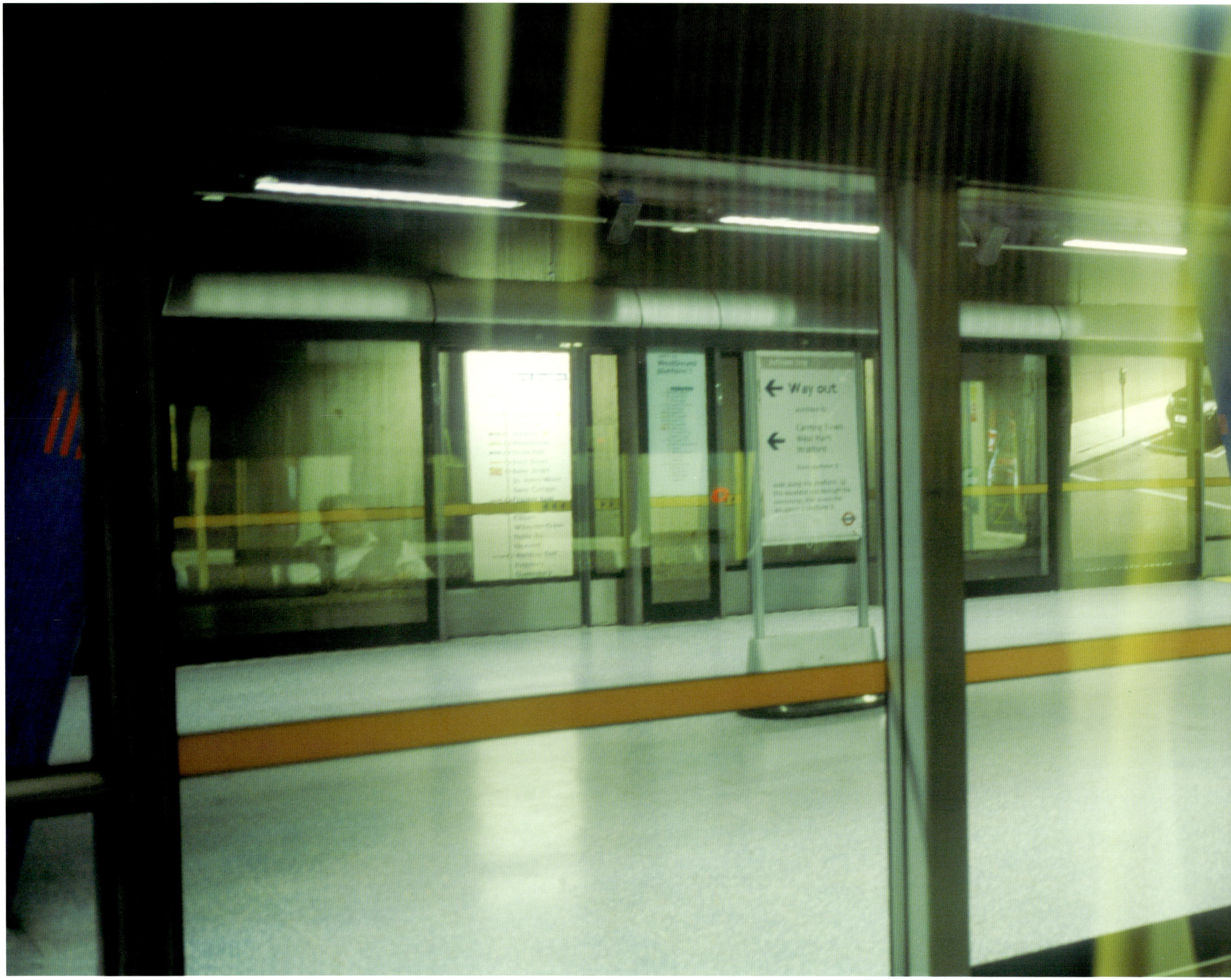

Station on the new Jubilee Line, London Underground

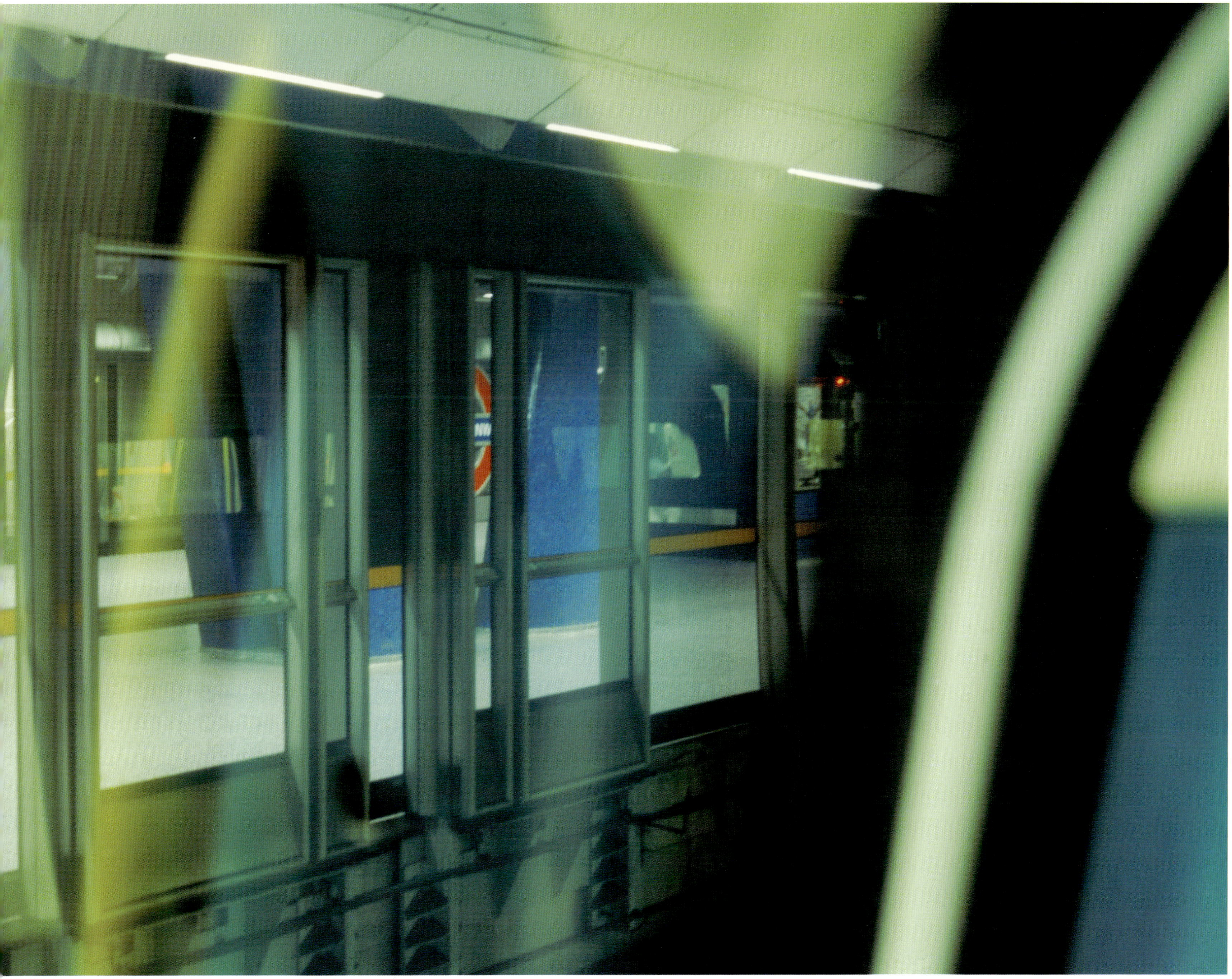

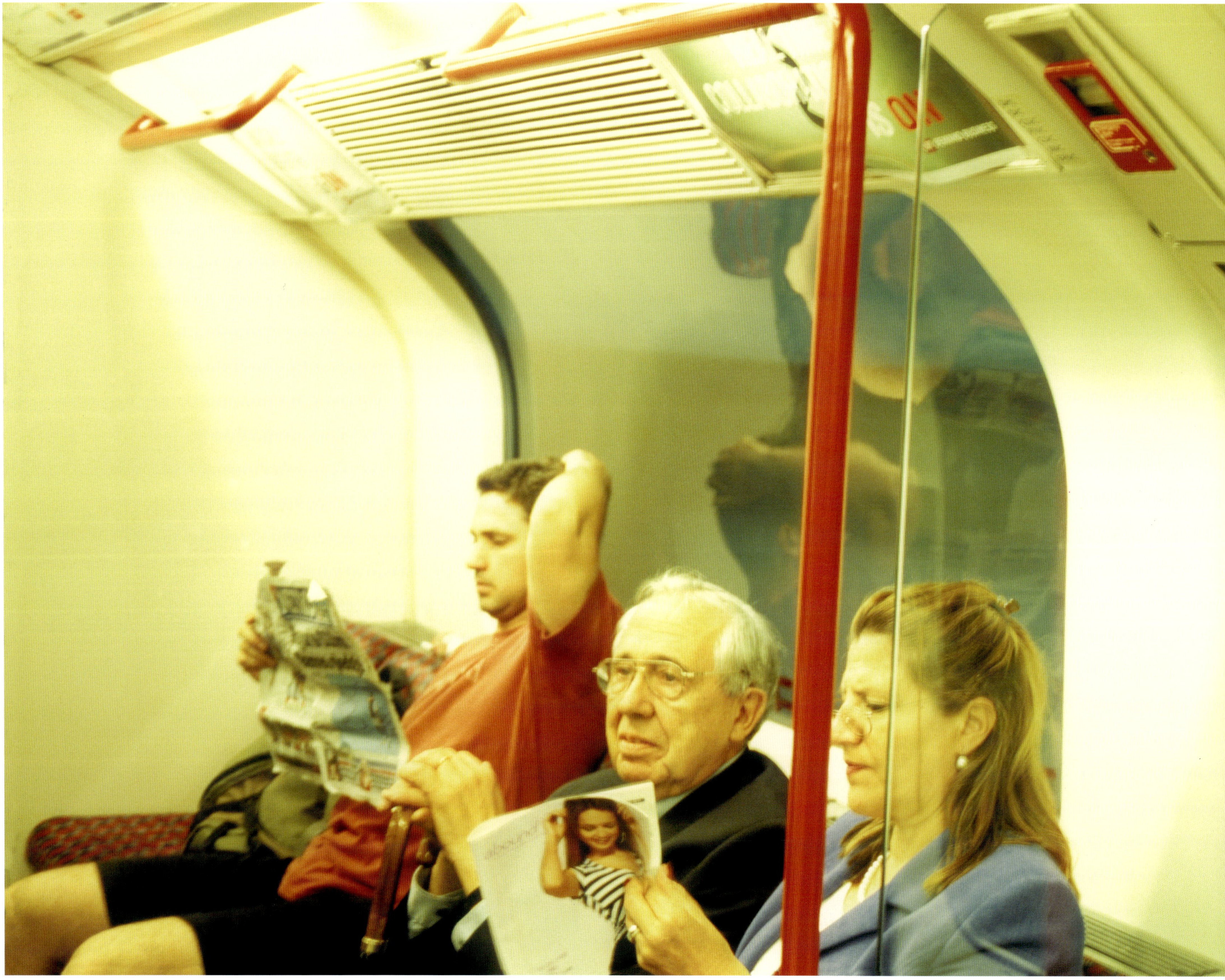

London Underground

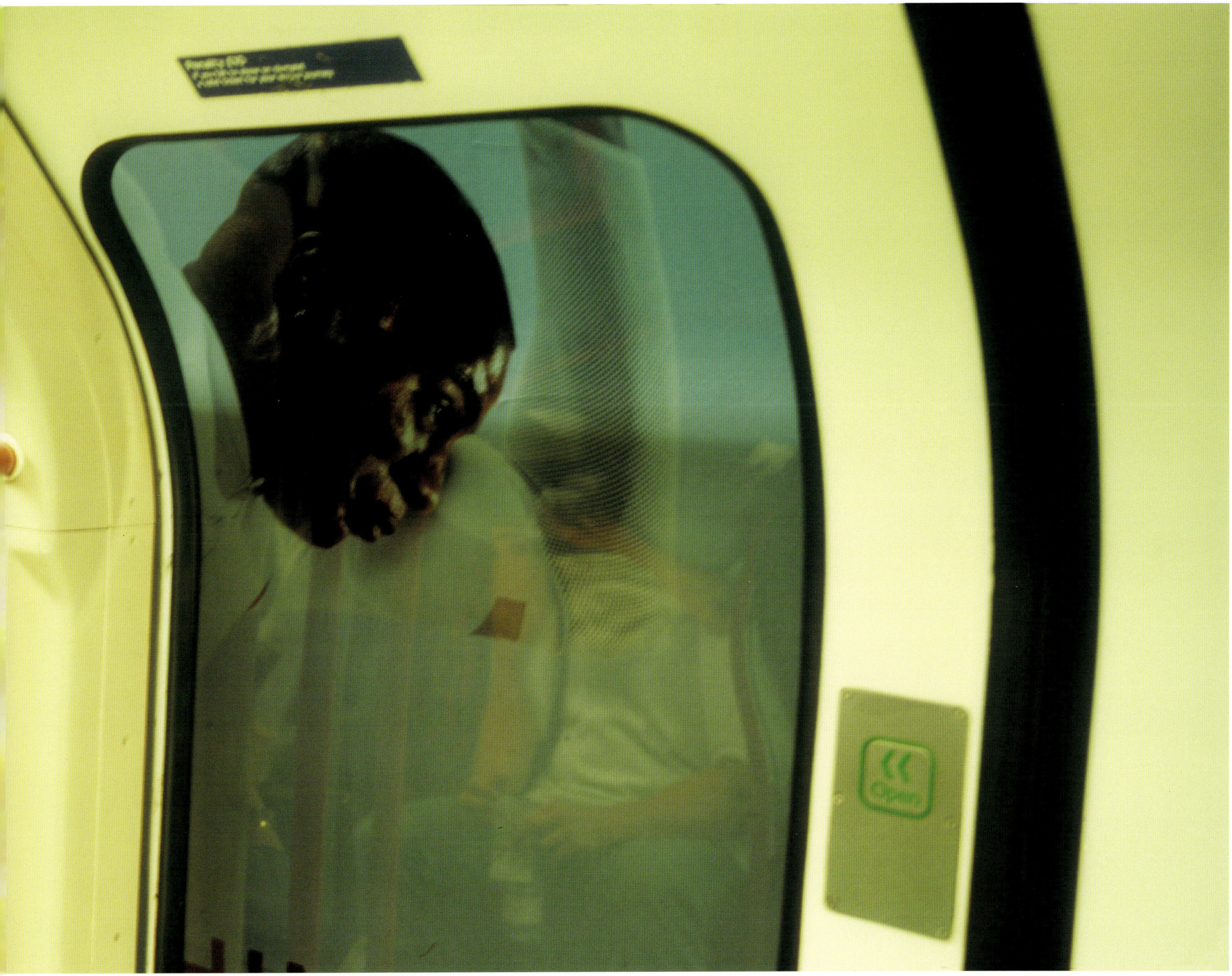
Open

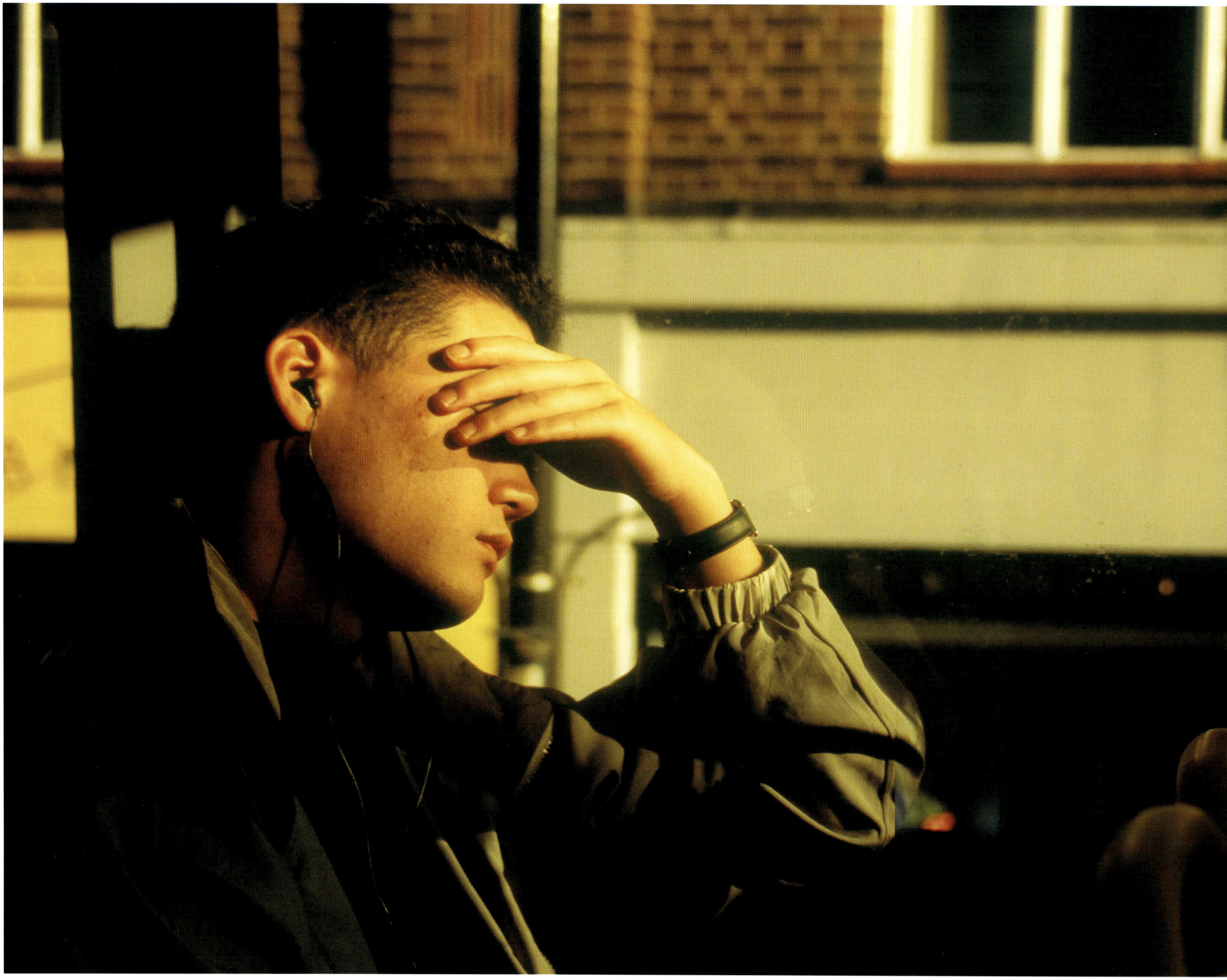

On the top deck of a London bus

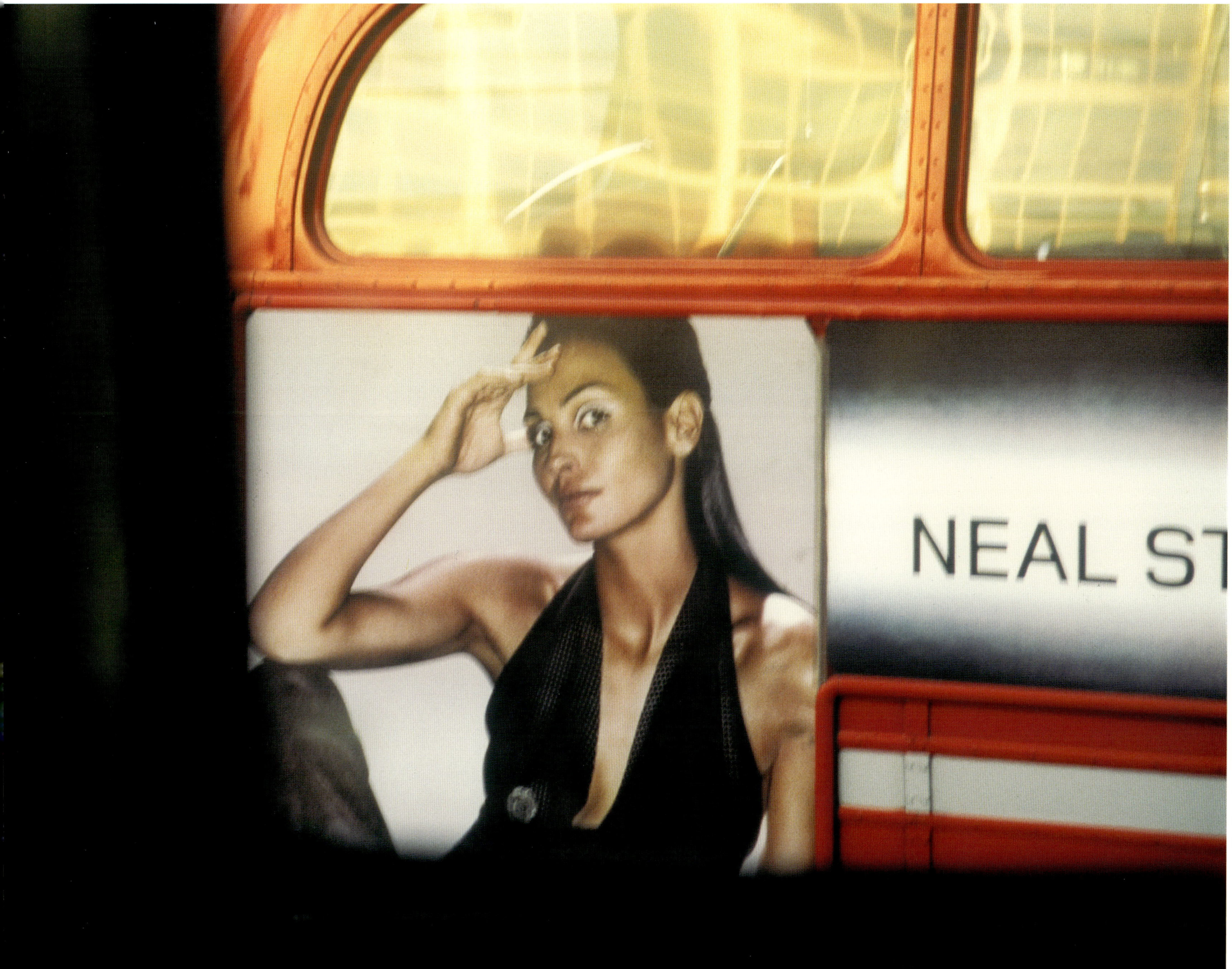
NEAL ST

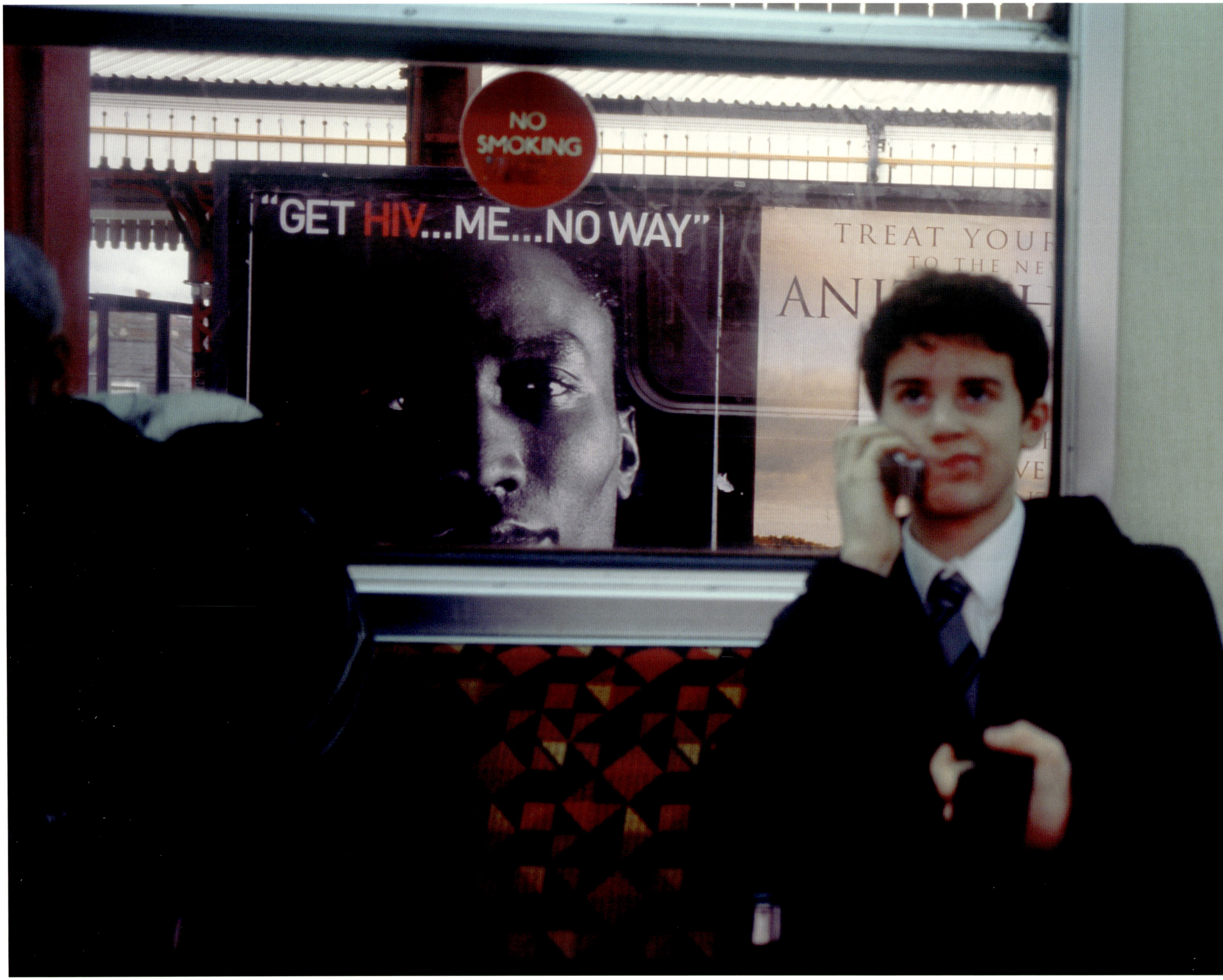

District Line, London Underground

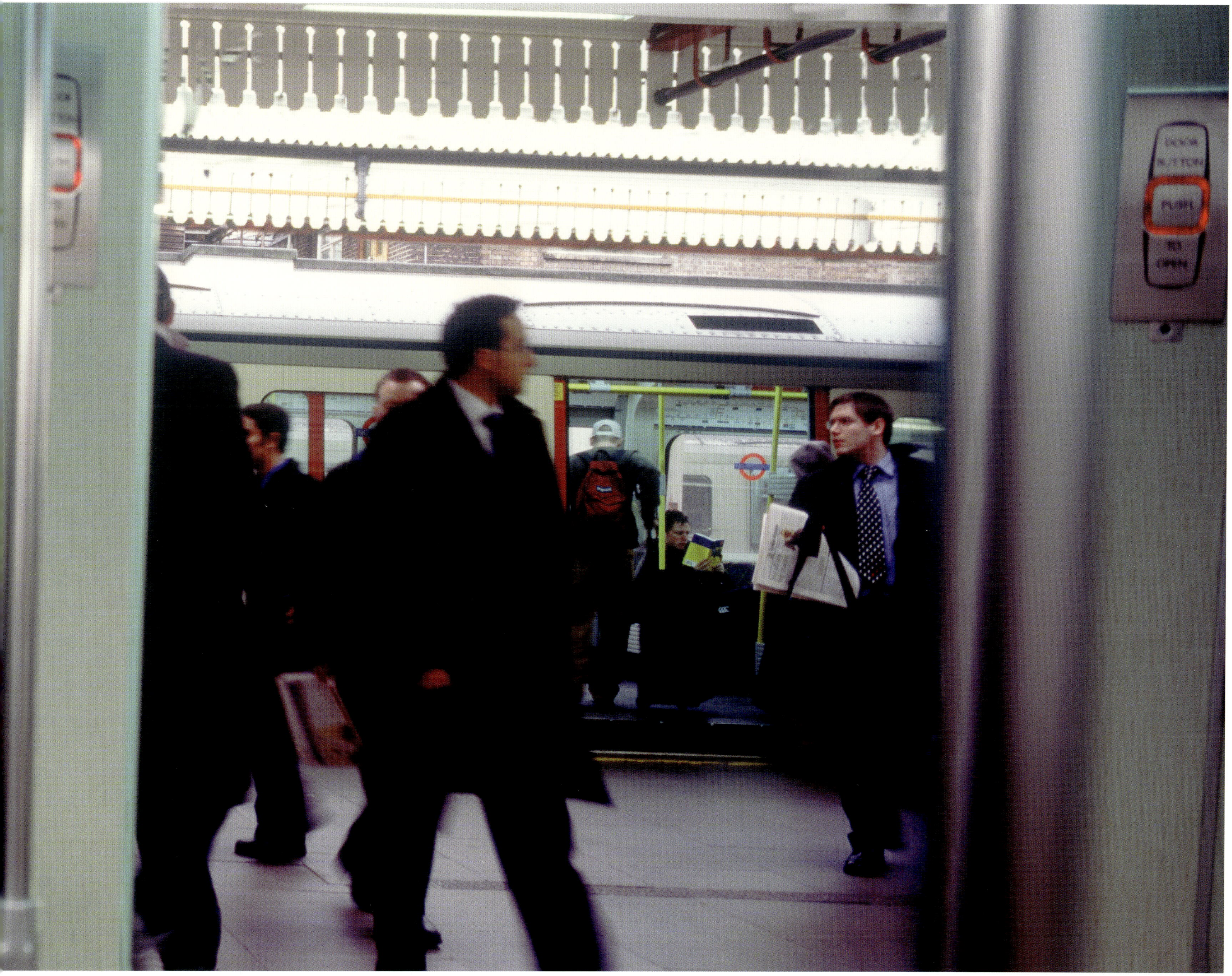
DOOR
BUTTON
PUSH
TO
OPEN

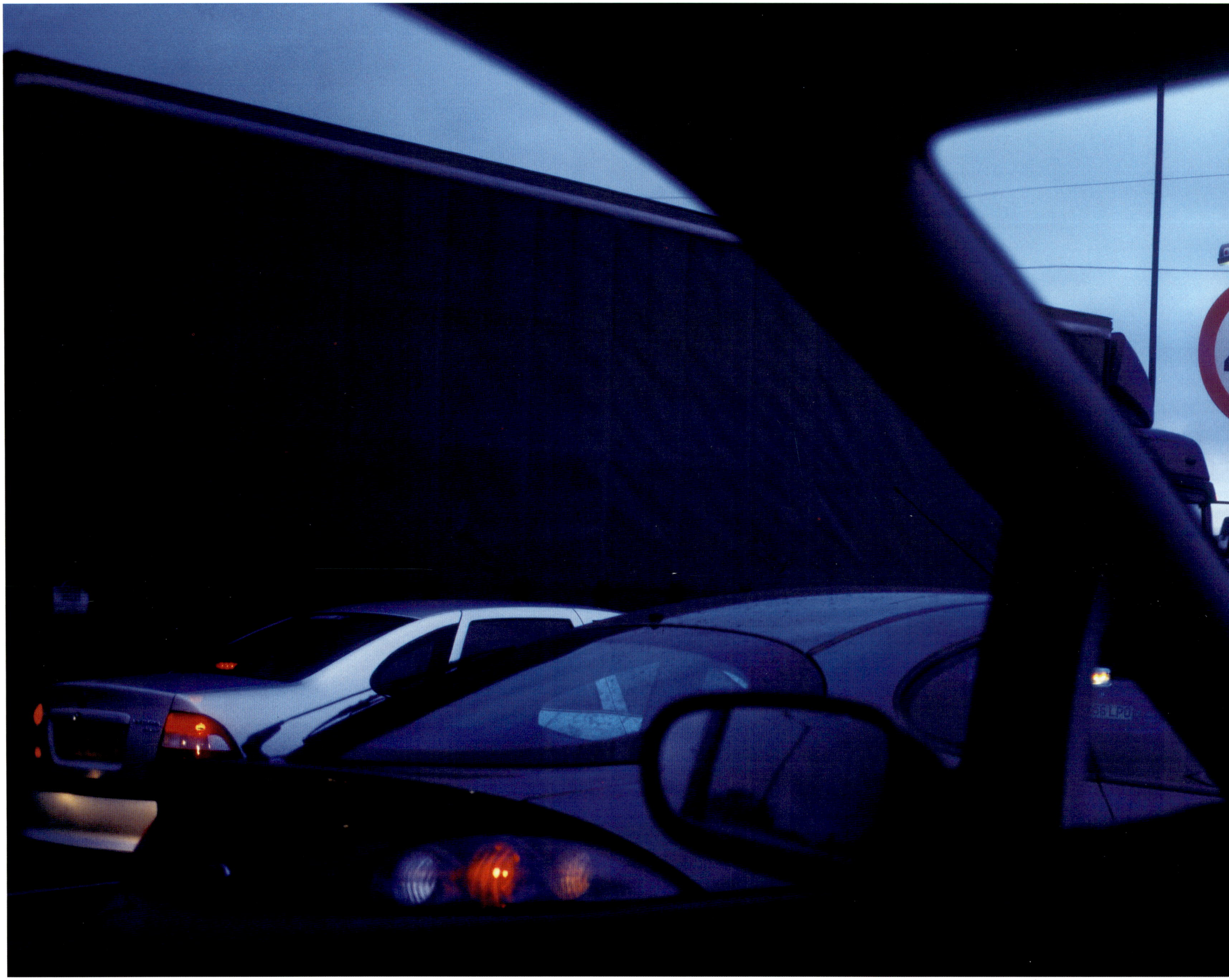

Going to London Heathrow

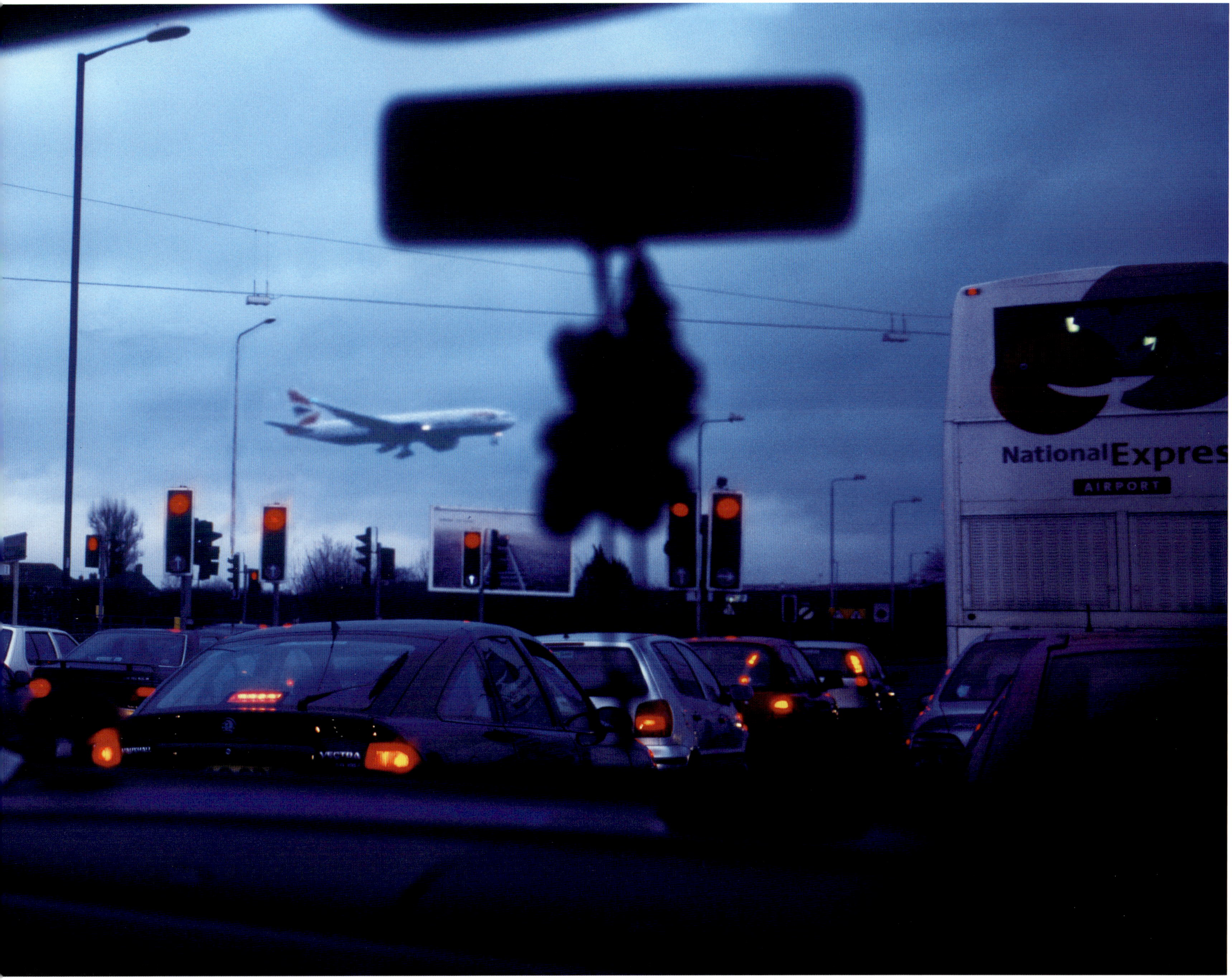
National Expres
AIRPORT
VECTRA

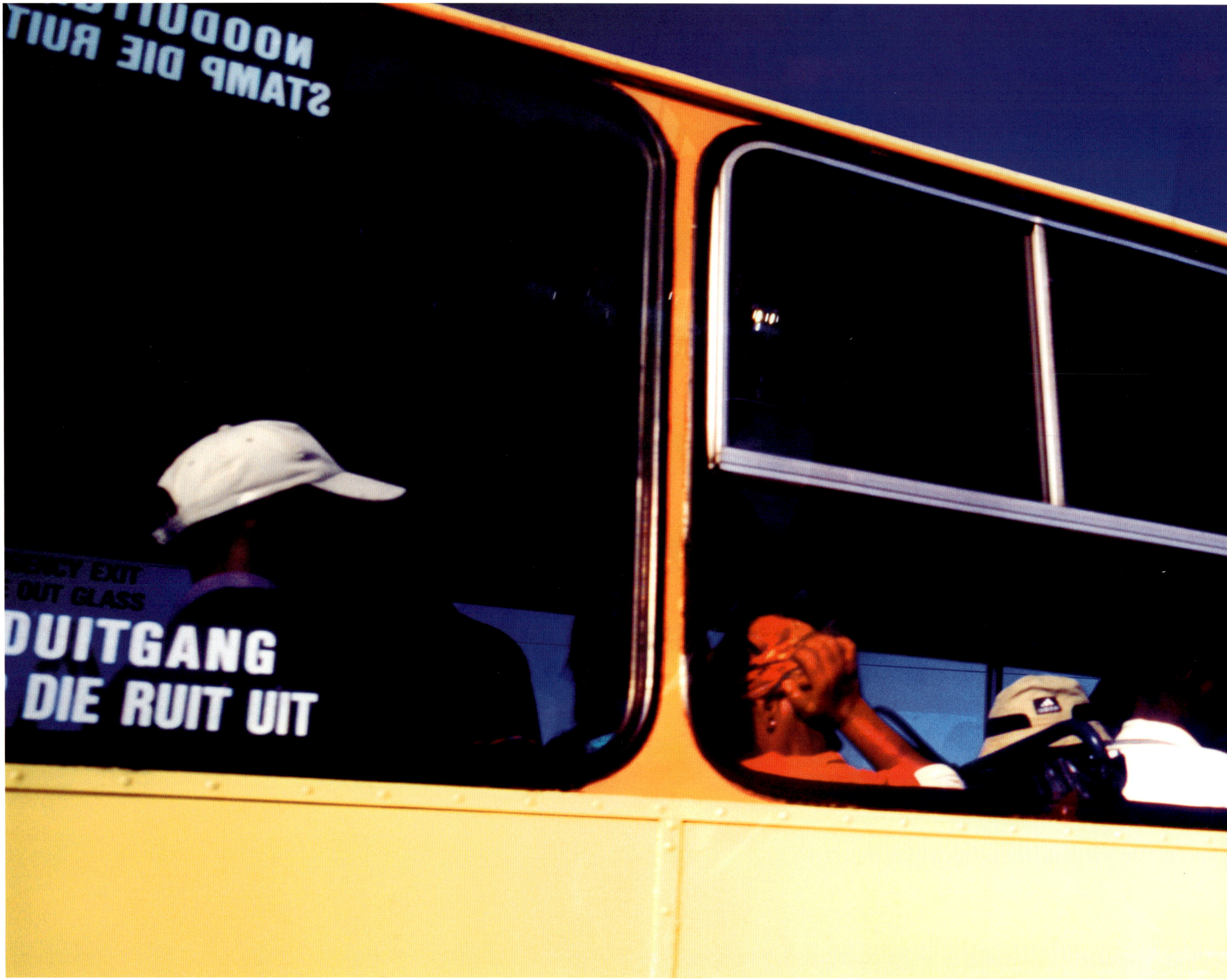

Bus in South Africa

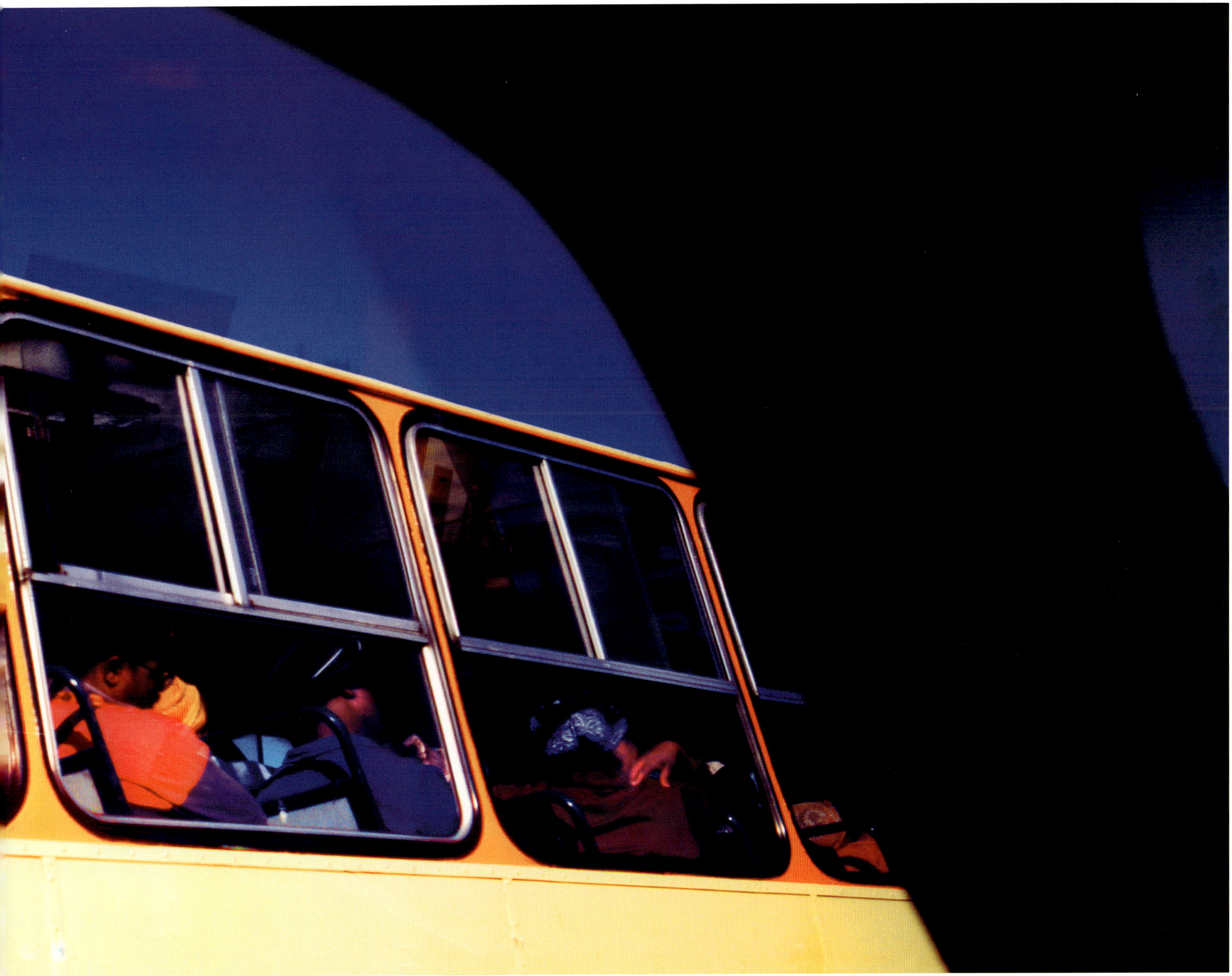

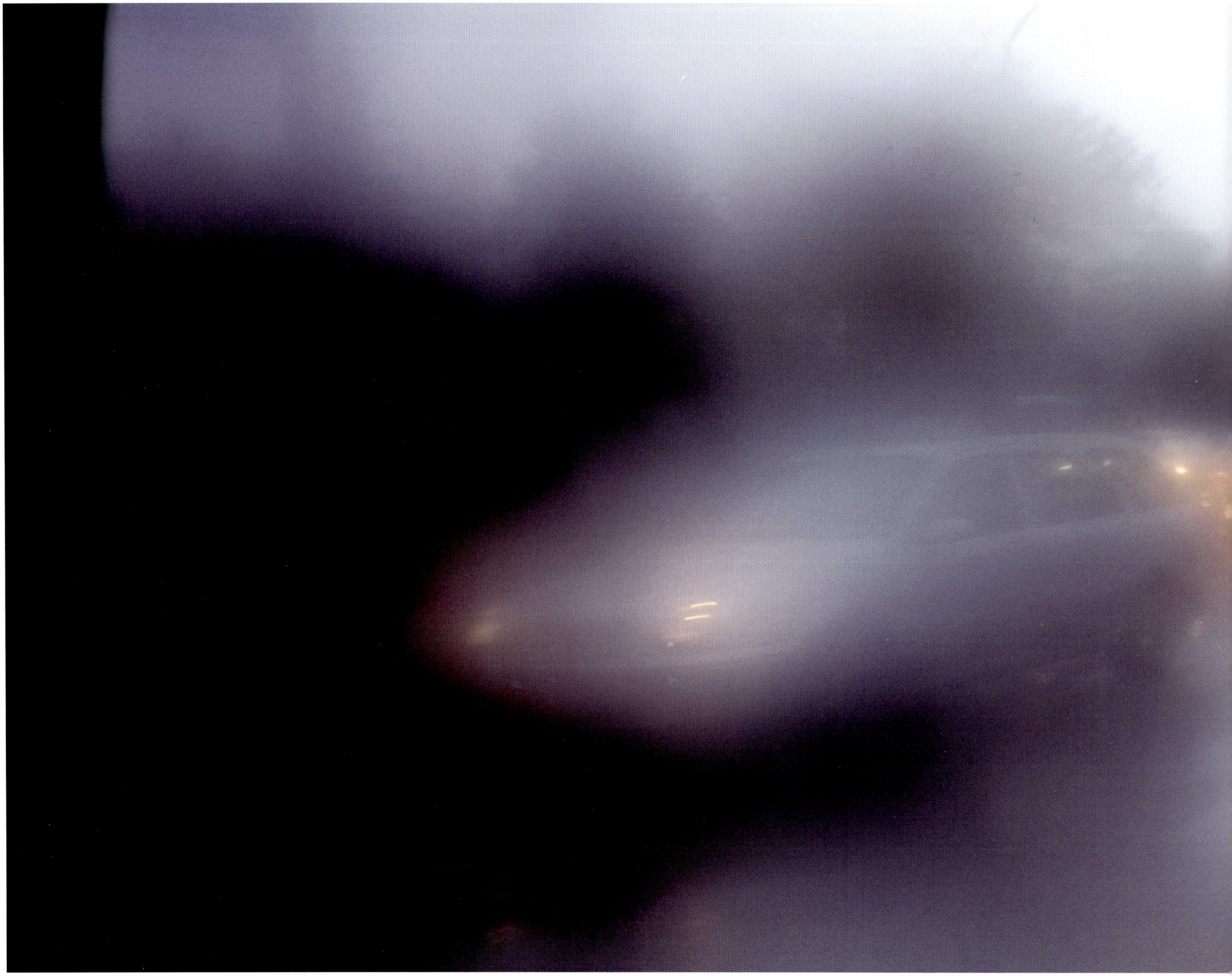

On the way to Lucca, Italy

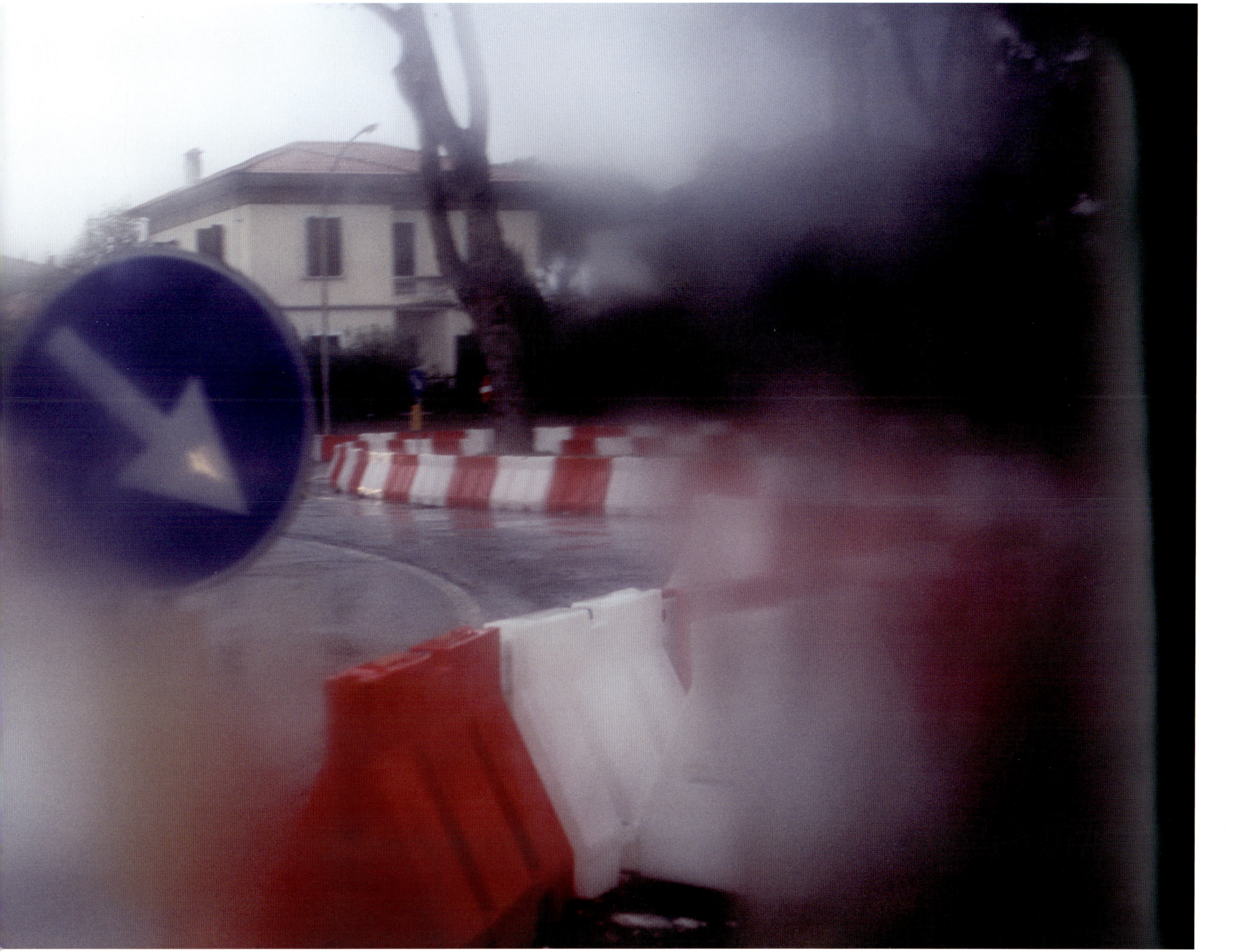

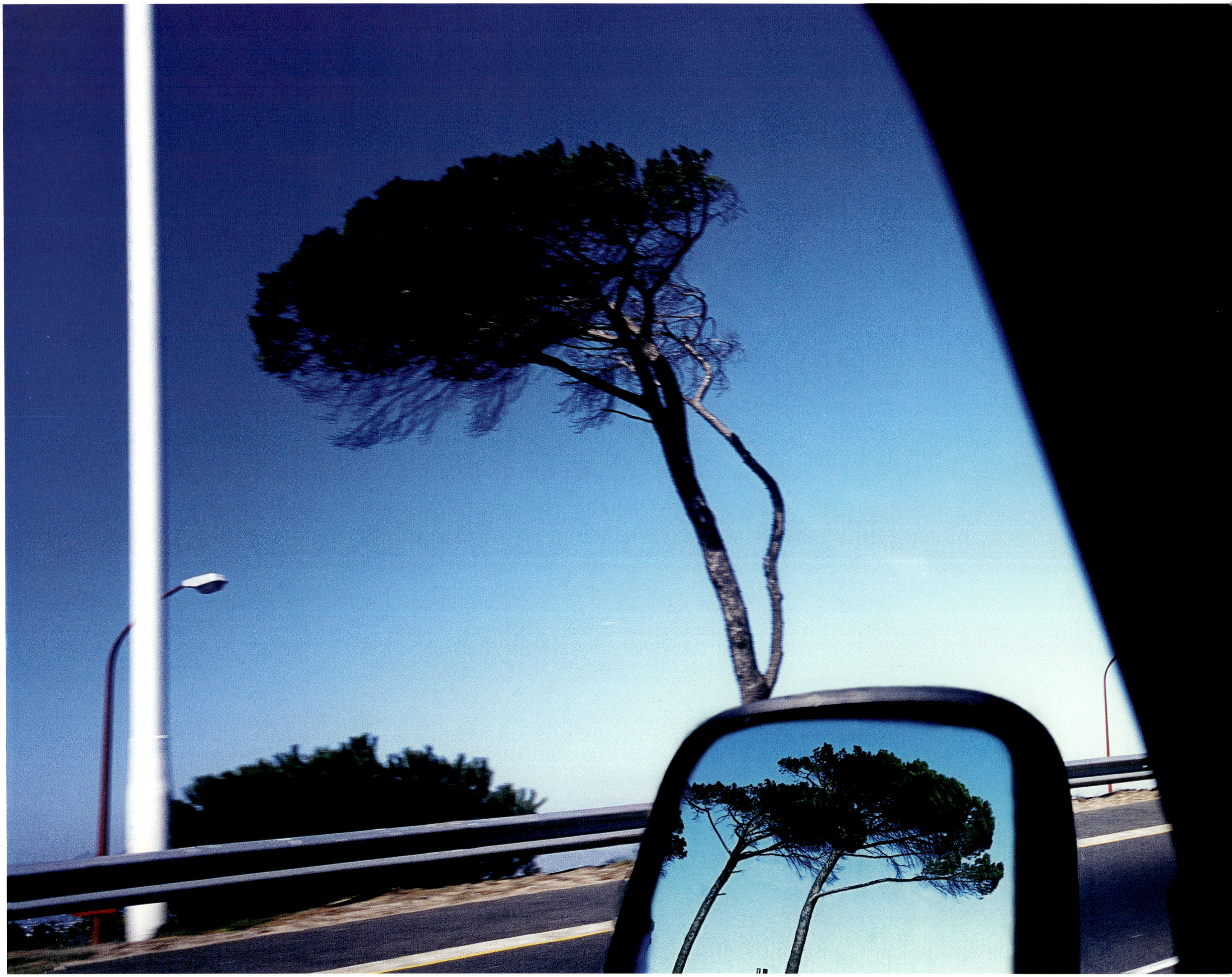

Mountain Highway, Cape Town, South Africa

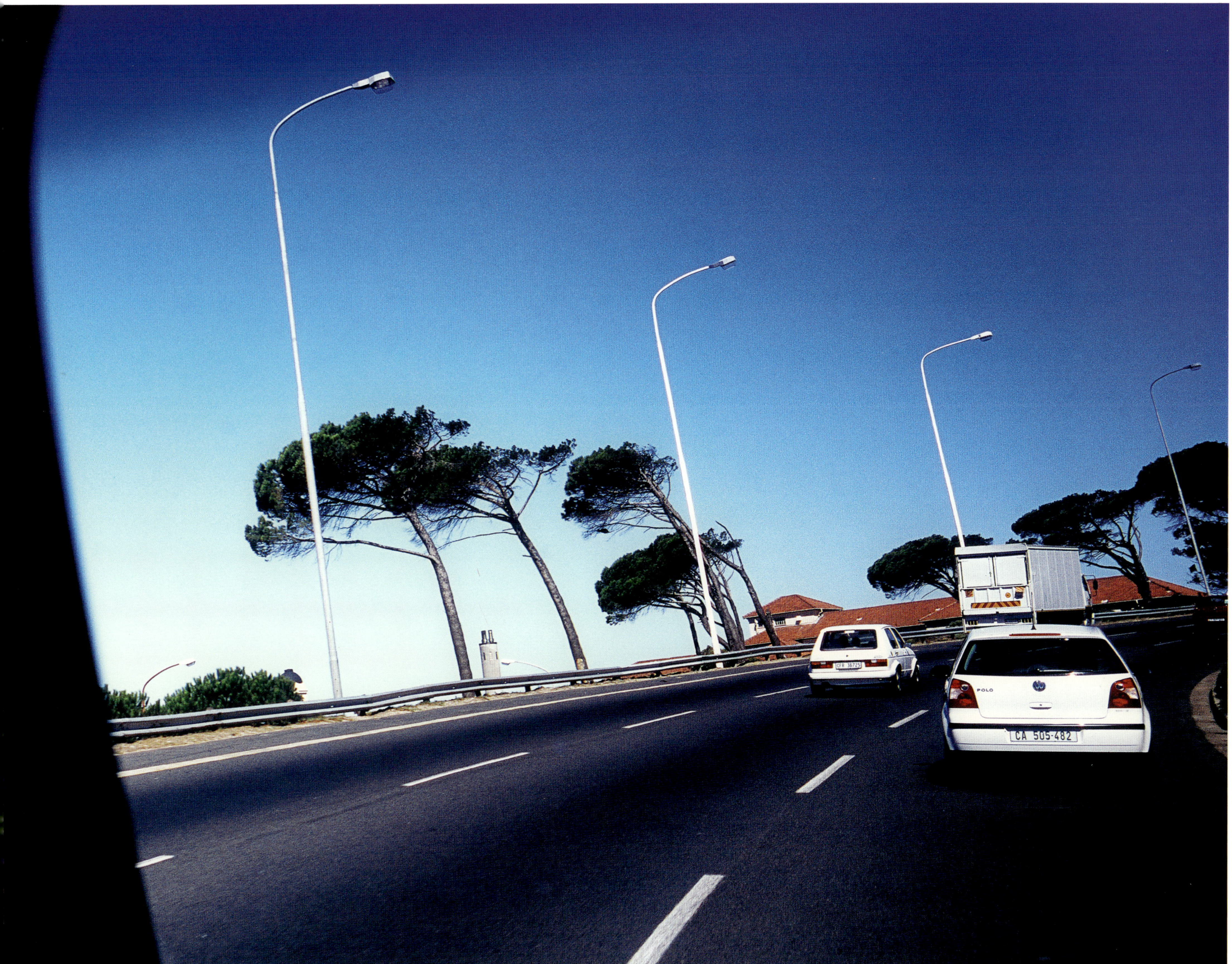
POLO
CA 505-482

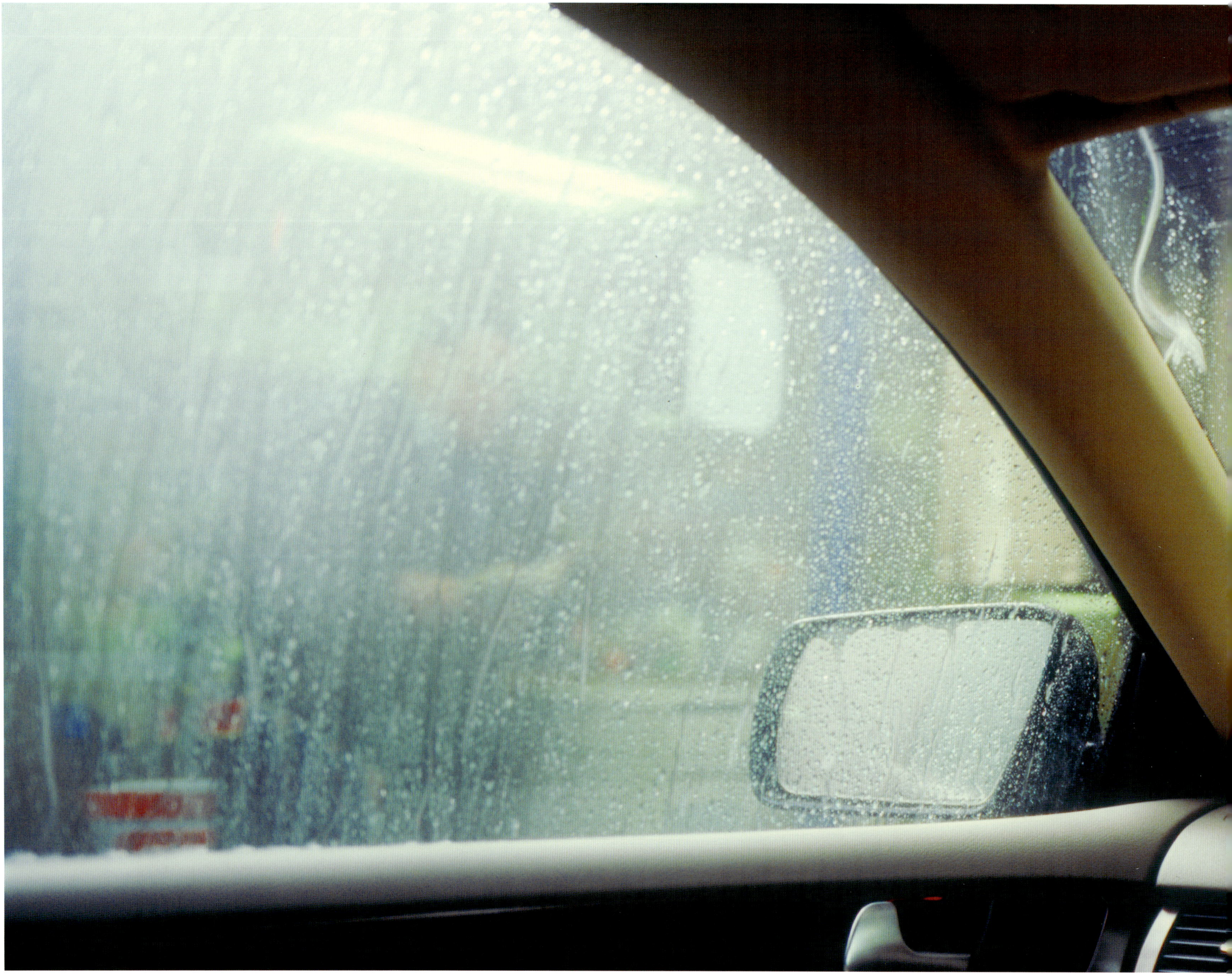

Carwash, London

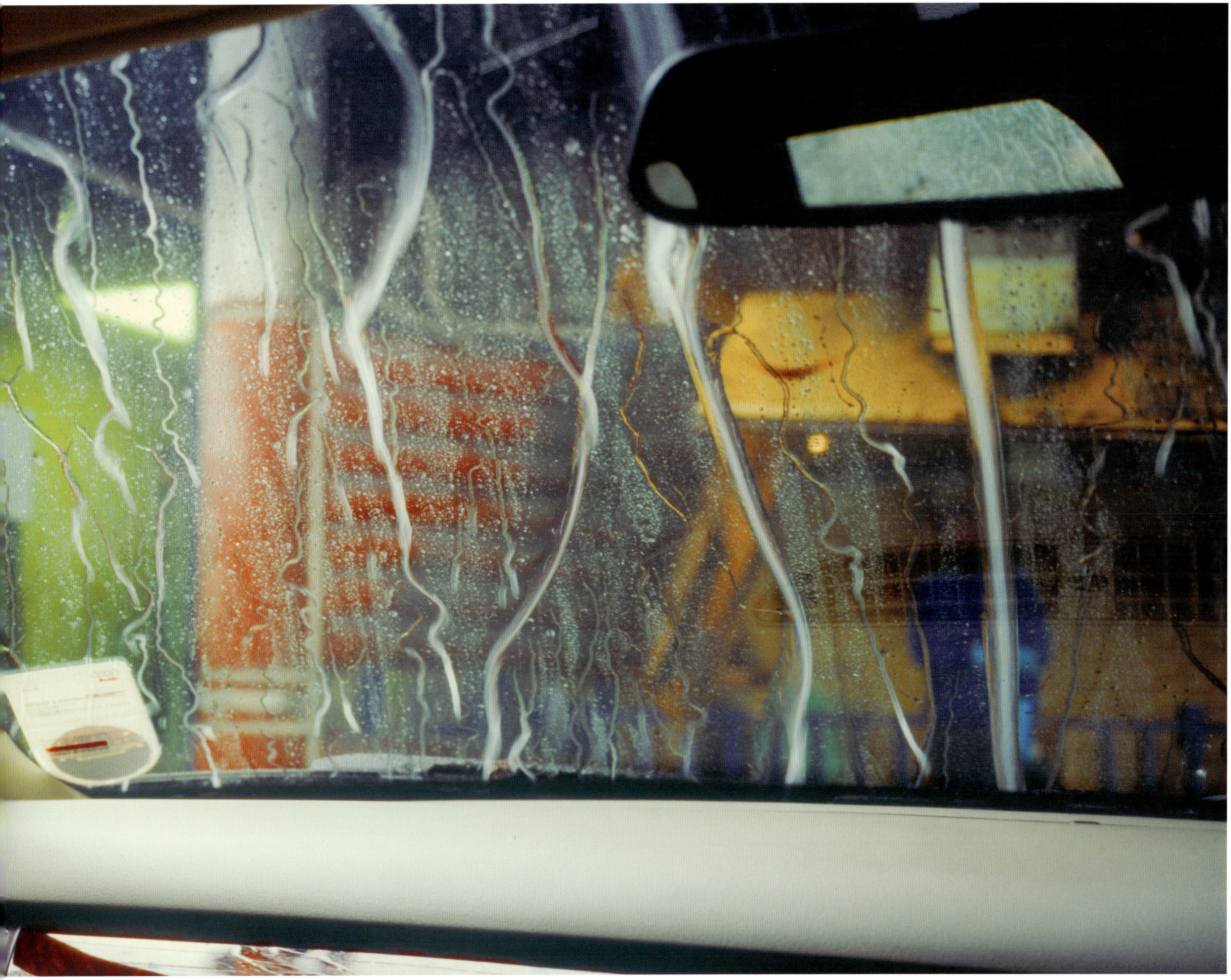

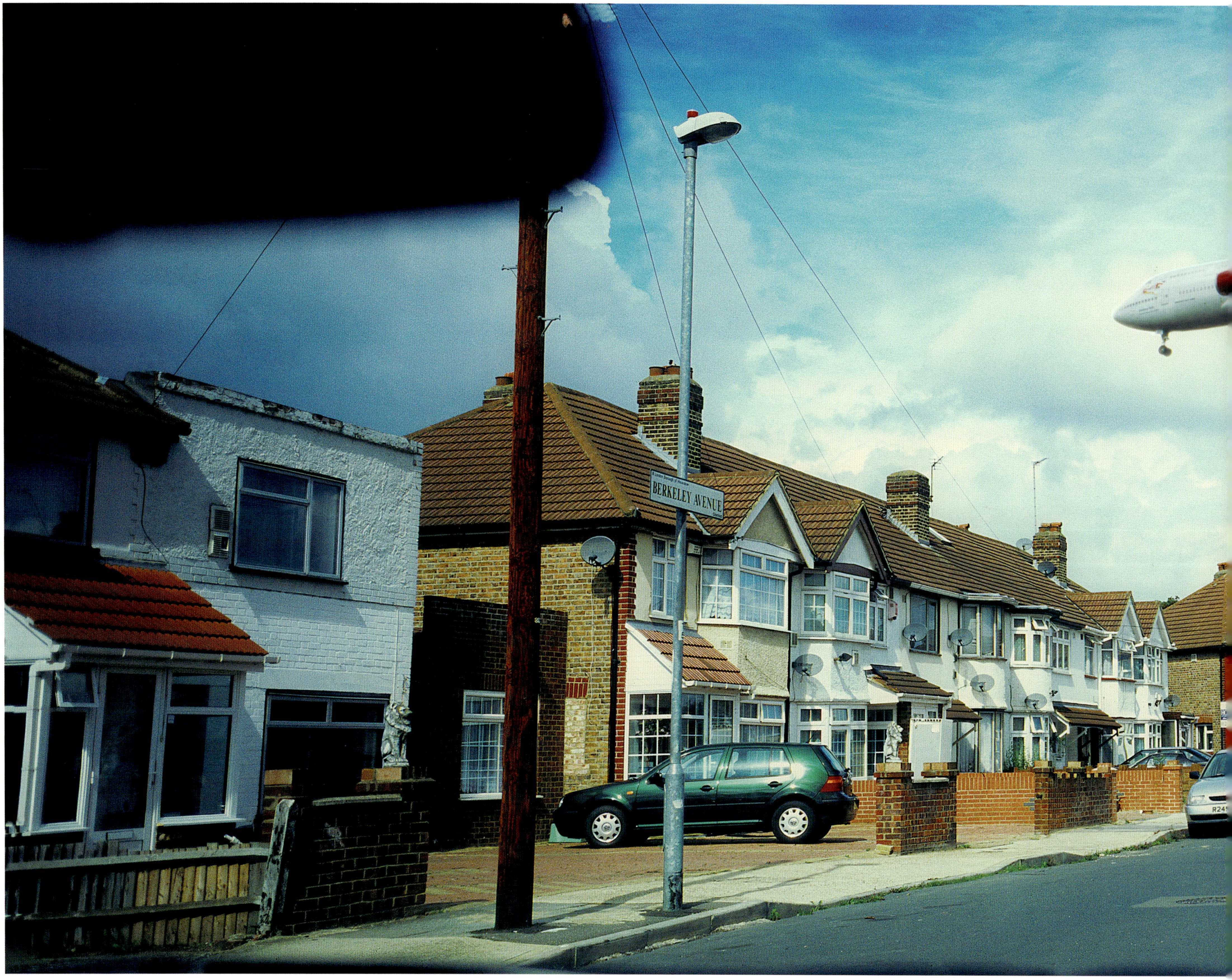

Berkeley Avenue, London Heathrow

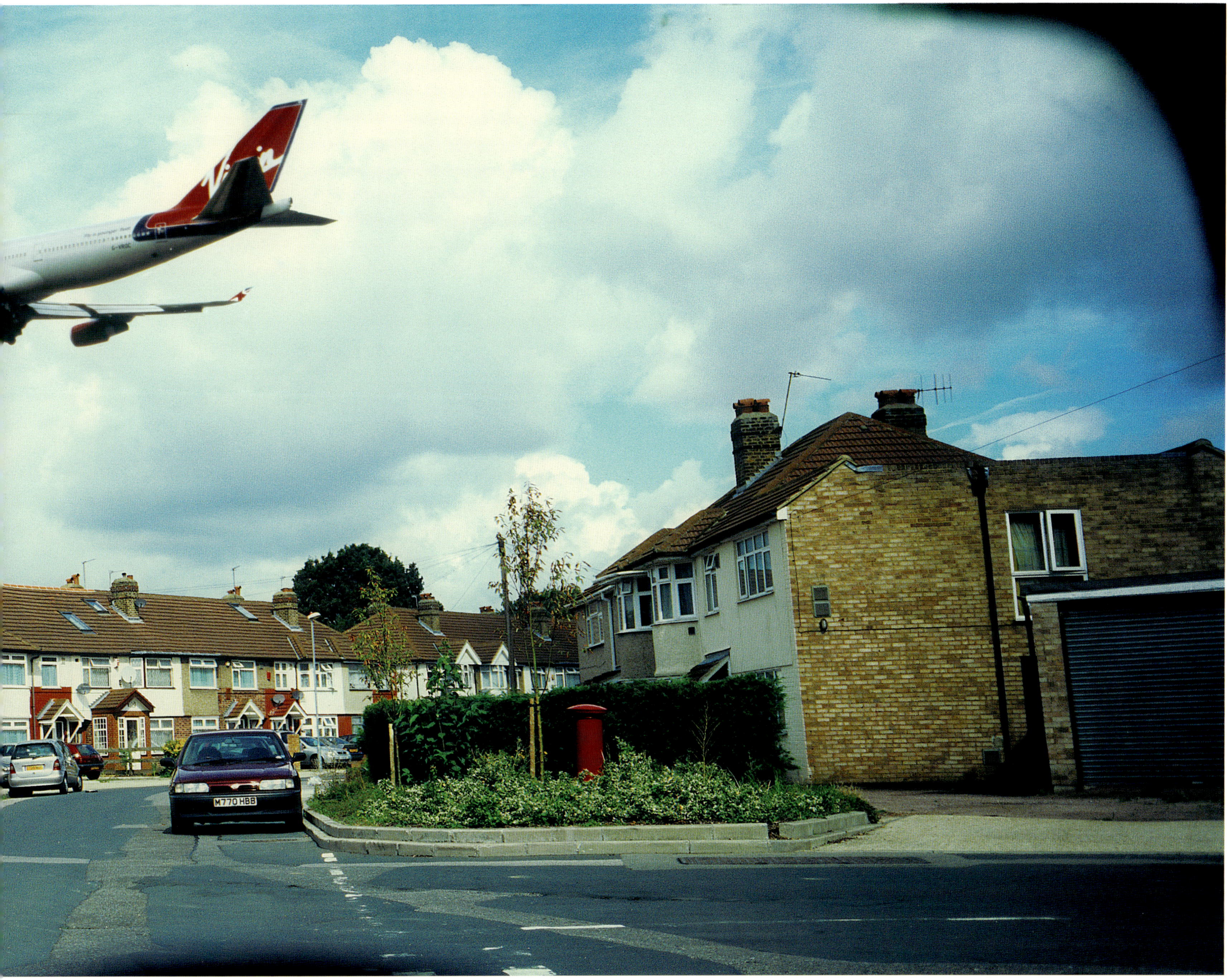
M770 HBB

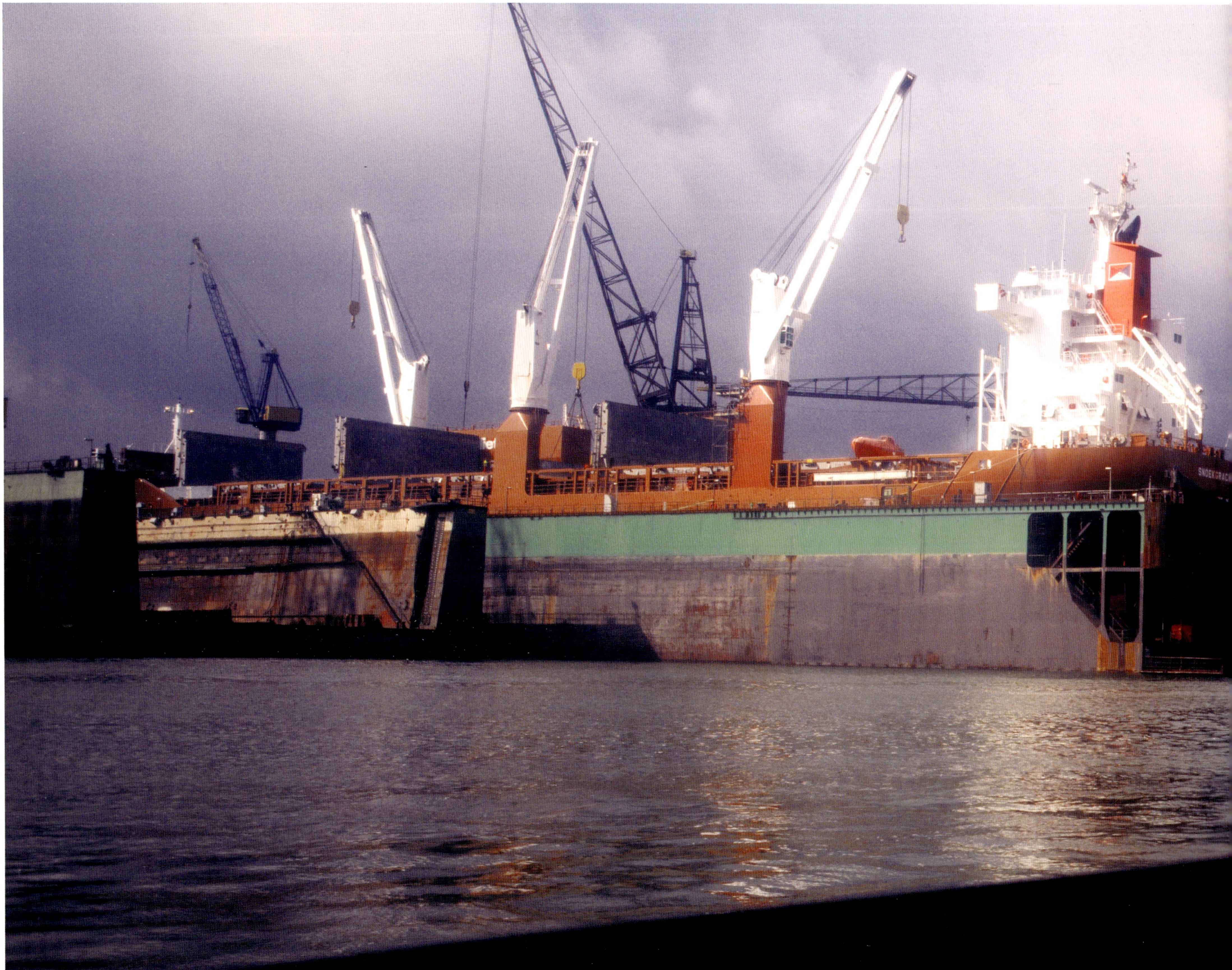

Rotterdam, Holland

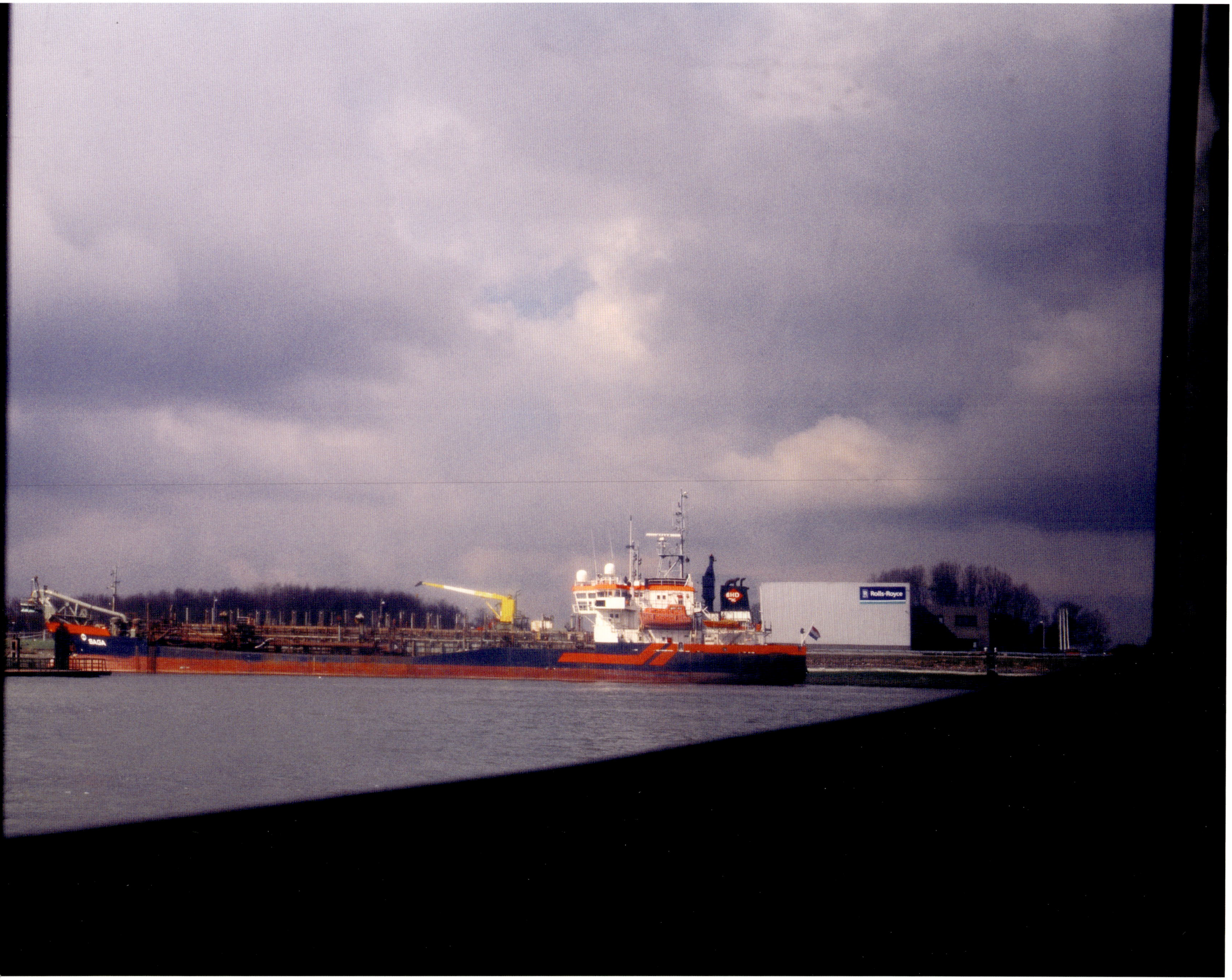
SAGA
BHD
Rolls-Royce

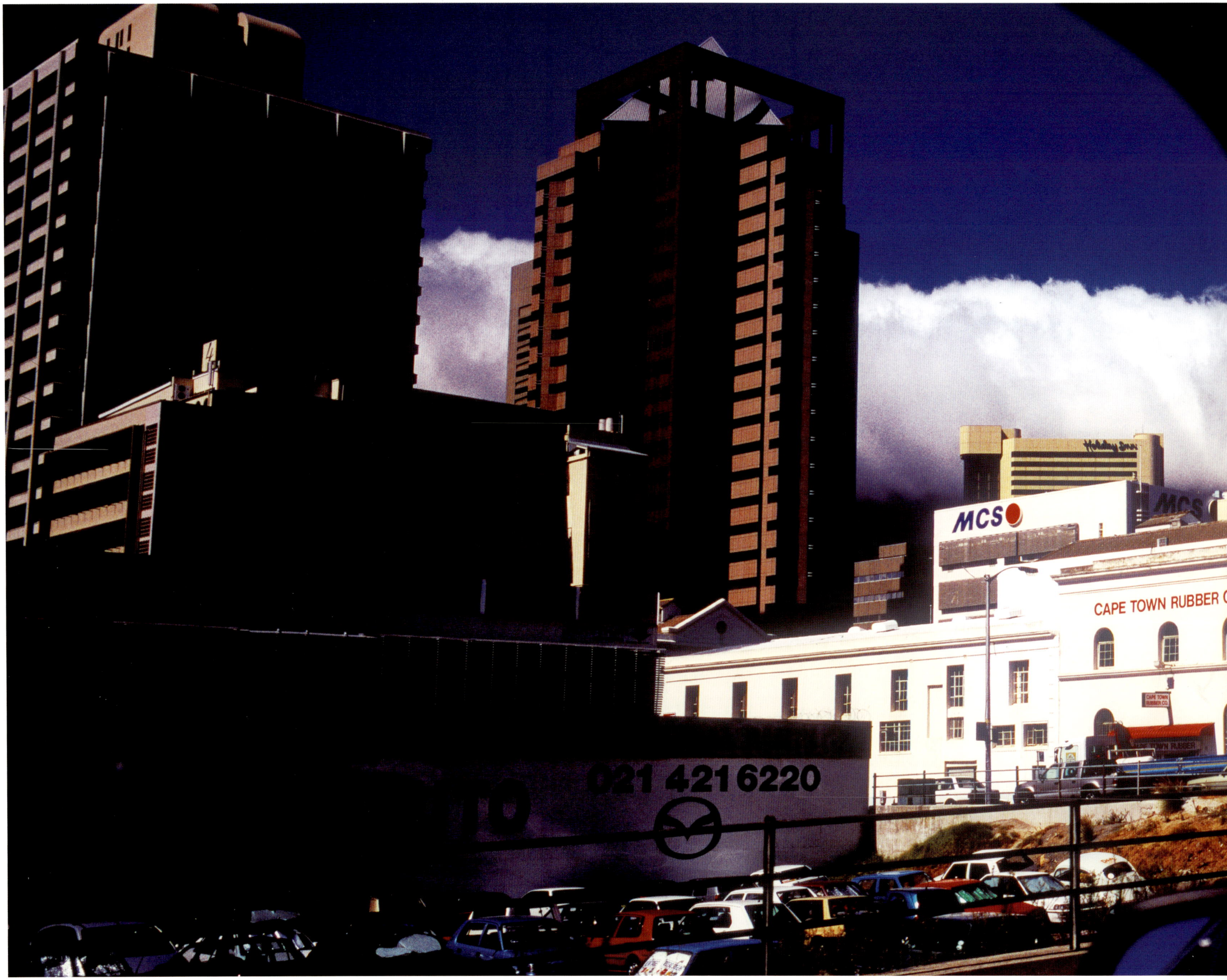

Cape Town, South Africa

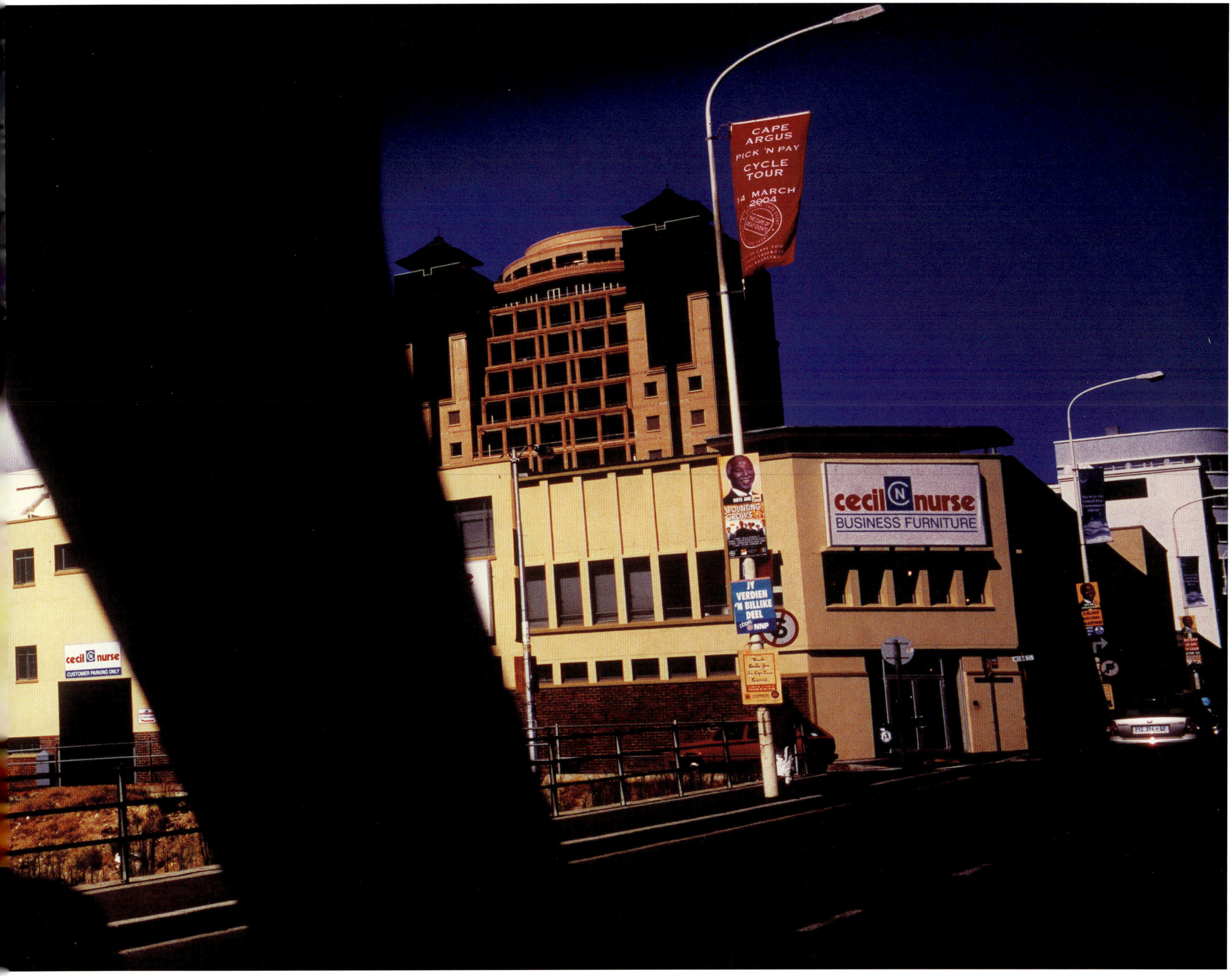
CAPE ARGUS
PICK 'N PAY
CYCLE TOUR
14 MARCH 2004
cecil nurse
BUSINESS FURNITURE
cecil nurse
CUSTOMER PARKING ONLY
JY VERDIEN 'N BILLIKE DEEL
stem NNP

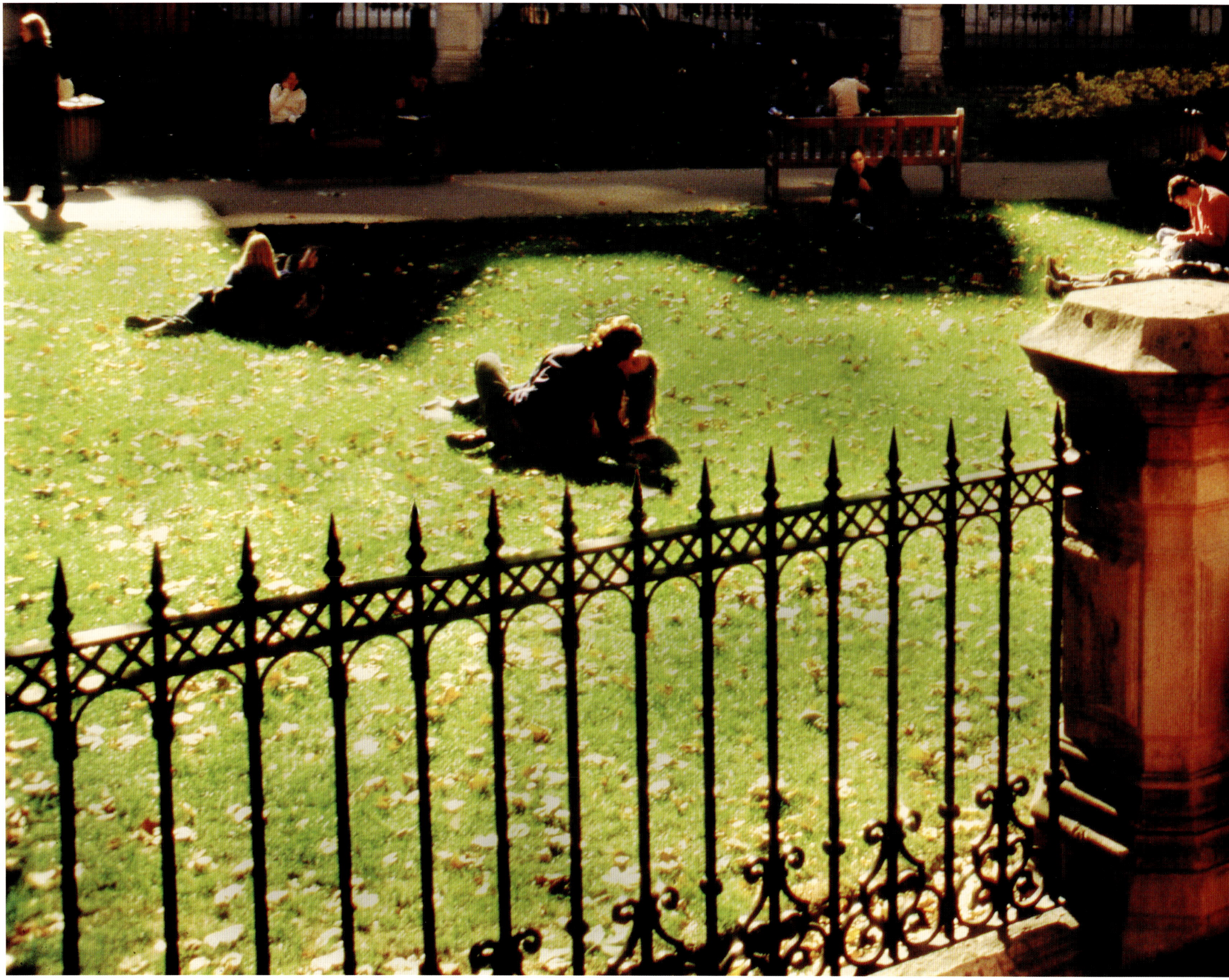

From the top of a bus in London

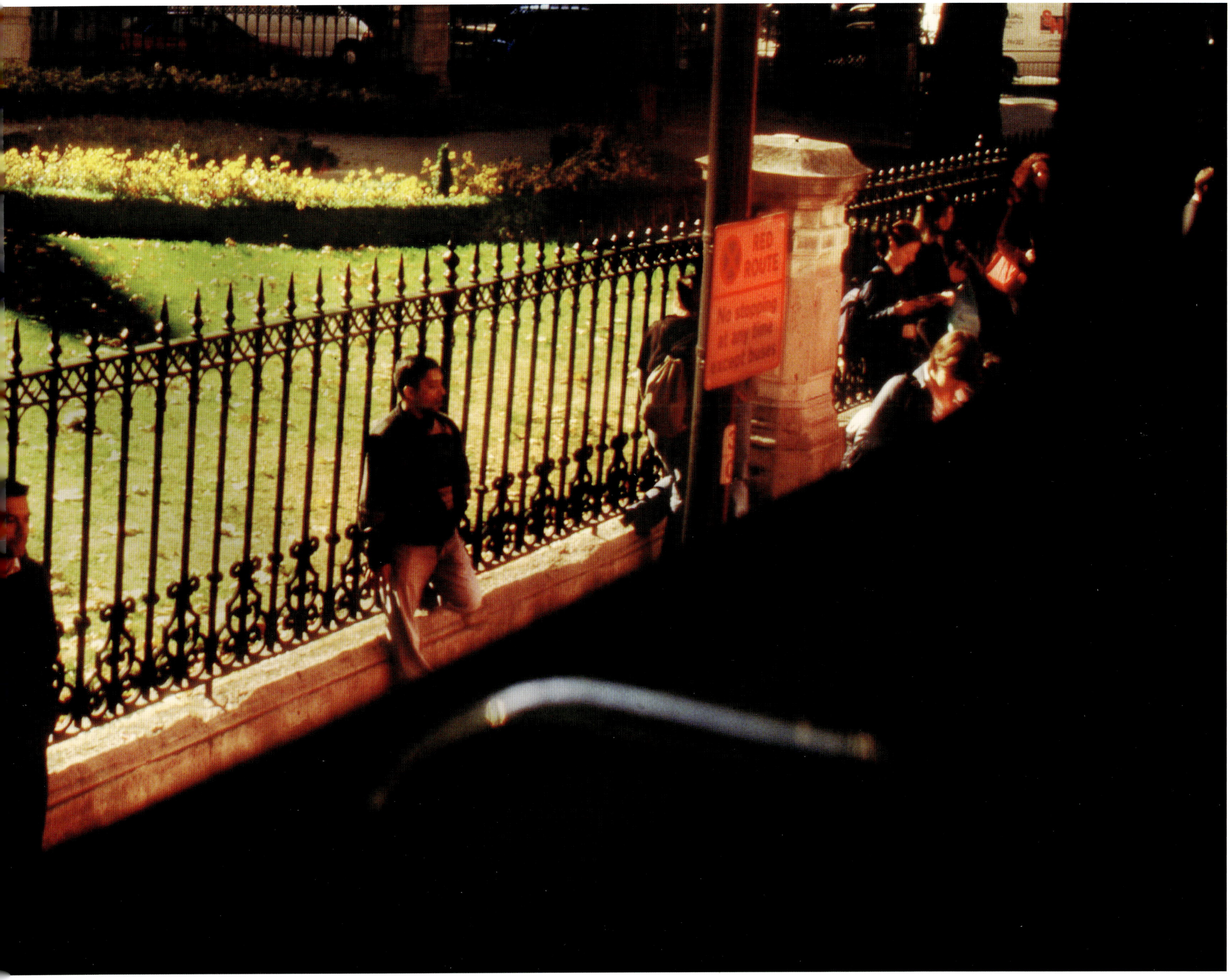
RED
ROUTE
No stopping
at any time
except buses

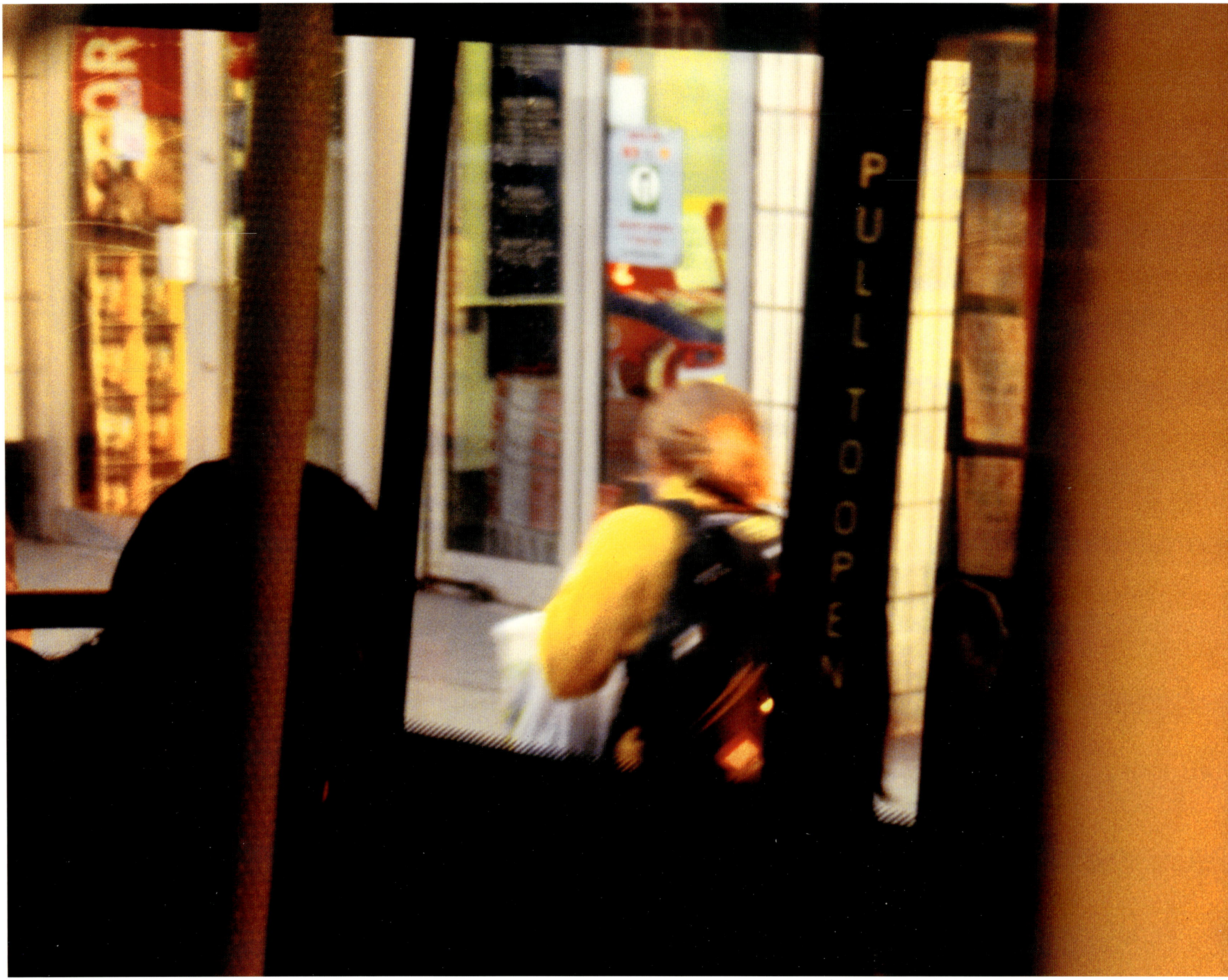

Bus stop London

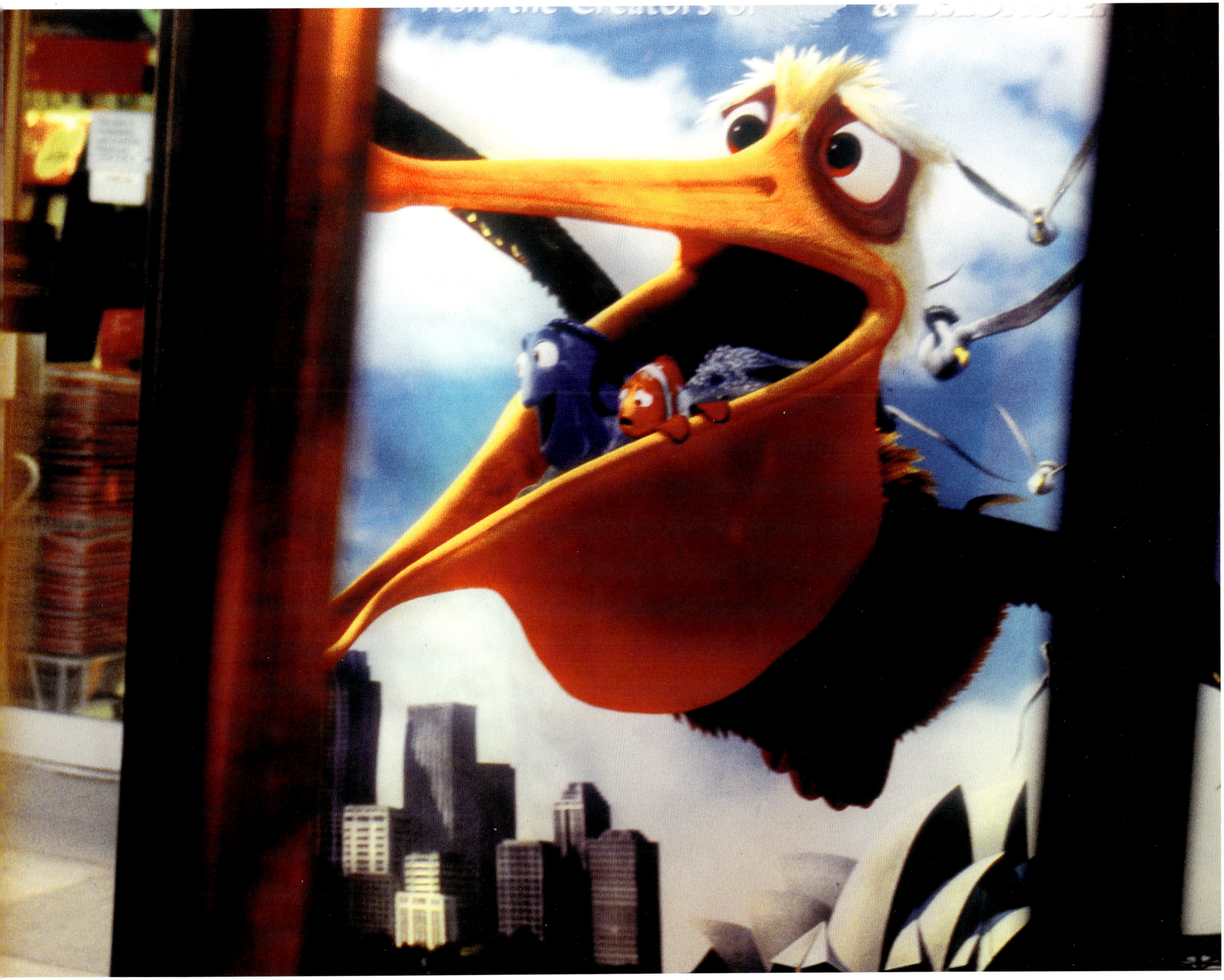

ACKNOWLEDGMENTS

My thanks to my wife Jane and my daughter Faye and son Luke whose unerring judgment has kept me on a straight path when my own was wavering, and my friends who have encouraged me with their support. And to the late John Gillard who showed me what an idea was.

Max Forsythe

Telephone: 44 (0) 20 8948 6888 email: max@maxforsythe.com

Website: maxforsythe.com

Design Frank Sully & Partners Limited

Telephone: 44 (0) 20 7267 9747 email: frank-sully@btconnect.com

First Published in 2004 by Booth-Clibborn Editions

12 Percy Street, London W1T 1DW, United Kingdom

www.booth-clibborn.com

A Cataloguing-in-Publication record for this book is available from the Publisher. ISBN 1-86154-278-X

Printed and bound in Italy by Grafiche Siz S.p.A.